Marx and Engels

A Conceptual Concordance

Gerard Bekerman

Marx and Engels:
A Conceptual Concordance

Translated by
Terrell Carver

BARNES & NOBLE BOOKS
TOTOWA, NEW JERSEY

© Presses Universitaires de France 1981
English edition first published 1983
Basil Blackwell Publisher Limited
108 Cowley Road, Oxford OX 4 1JF, England
First published in the USA 1983 by
BARNES & NOBLE BOOKS
81 ADAMS DRIVE
TOTOWA, NEW JERSEY, 07512

Library of Congress Cataloging in Publication Data

Bekerman, Gérard.
    Marx and Engles, a conceptual concordance.

    Translation of: Vocabulaire de marxisme.
    English and German.
    Includes index.
    1. Communism—Dictionaries. 2. Marx, Karl, 1818–1883
—Languages—Glossaries, etc. 3. Marx, Karl, 1818–1883
—Concordances. 4. Engels, Friedrich, 1820–1895—Language
—Glossaries, etc. 5. Engels, Friedrich, 1820–1895—Concordances.
6. English language—Dictionaries—German. 7. German
Language—Dictionaries—English.
I. Title.
HX17.B4313, 1983 335.4′03′21 83–11931

ISBN 0–389–20427–7

Printed in Great Britain

CONTENTS

ACKNOWLEDGEMENTS

The Translator and Publisher are grateful for permission to use extracts from the following copyright editions:

Frederick Engels: *Anti-Dühring*, Lawrence & Wishart; *Dialectics of Nature*, Lawrence & Wishart.

Karl Marx: *Capital*, Lawrence & Wishart; *Capital*, Penguin Books Ltd and Random House Inc.; *Contribution to the Critique of Political Economy*, Lawrence & Wishart; *Grundrisse*, Penguin Books Ltd and Random House Inc.; *Theories of Surplus Value*, Lawrence & Wishart.

Karl Marx and Frederick Engels: *Collected Works*, Lawrence & Wishart; *Selected Works in One Volume*, Lawrence & Wishart.

TRANSLATOR'S PREFACE

I have adapted Gérard Bekerman's *Vocabulaire du Marxisme/Wörter-buch des Marxismus* (Presses Universitaires de France, Paris, 1981) for the English reader, using the most readily available English translations, English-language original texts where appropriate and my own translations where necessary. Marx and Engels have had many English translators, so there are inevitable inconsistencies in terminology and some uneven results. I have taken the *Conceptual Concordance* to be a guide to the ideas of Marx and Engels as they appear in standard English editions, rather than a collection of extracts translated just as I would have them. I urge the reader to pursue each passage back to its context, using the references provided, and to study the Table of Entries, as cross-referencing can never be fully comprehensive.

I am grateful to the staff of the University Library, Bristol, for their help in obtaining German and English source material.

Bristol   Terrell Carver

FOREWORD

The centenary of Marx's death is an appropriate time to present *A Conceptual Concordance* to the works of Marx and Engels. My return to the works themselves was stimulated not only by the task of removing obscurities in interpretation but also by something much more fundamental. In order to recover Marx as he was it is necessary to separate him from partisan strife and self-contradictory doctrines. To hear Marx correctly, to comprehend him as precisely as possible, to find in the text what he actually said, rather than what he has been made to say, we must forget subsequent Marxisms. To understand Marx we must depart from earlier critics and get down to the truth, even to weak spots and limitations. A hundred years have passed without freeing Marx's works from the innumerable interpretations which have often submerged them in contradictions. The drive to criticize and clarify has had the result that Marx has been less *understood* than *used*. He has been interpreted rather less through his own works than through an imputed relation to the thought-systems and influential ideas of our own time, and he has been used less for his own sake than for a recasting of his works into a political ideology. The critics have won in breadth what they have lost in depth. In a certain sense they discovered the origin of Marxism, but not in the ideas of Marx.[1]

A clear focus on Marx's work is difficult to achieve so long as different Marxist ideologies – whether political or academic in origin – put up such stiff resistance. With Theodor Adorno and

---

1. In their correspondence Marx and Engels always used the expression 'Marxist' in inverted commas. The statement, 'All I know is that I am not a Marxist' (*SC* 415), was not written down by Marx himself. In fact, it was Engels who transcribed this remark. According to Engels, Marx made this 'confession' in 1882, a year before his death, during the rise of self-styled Marxist tendencies in French socialism. There is in Marx's and Engels's works a marked scruple concerning the use of the word 'Marxism'. For example Engels wrote 'The Marxist Congress . . .' and immediately commented, 'I use this term for brevity' (*Werke* 22.71). Engels also criticized the 'Marxophobia' of the 'Possibilist' Benoît Malon (1841–93) (*Werke* 35.239). It is interesting to note that Engels recalled his friend's confession after Marx's death to Paul Lafargue (27 August 1890), to Conrad Schmidt (5 August 1890) – and during Marx's lifetime to Eduard Bernstein (2/3 November 1882).

Jürgen Habermas, German philosophy has again – so far as language is concerned – adopted neo-Hegelian idealism. Between German philosophy and structuralism, which has been of such importance in France over the last sixty years, we find good deal of common ground. When Marxism lives, Marx is dead. Which interpretations can we trust? Which Marxism respects the ideas of Marx? Which comes closest to them? Which departs from them? Never were Marxists further from a real understanding of Marx's works. Debate has triumphed over science. This has happened without influencing historical events or diminishing international conflict; on the contrary, it has assisted the growth of new Marxisms perhaps more accessible, more subtle, less self-assured. But where is Marx in all this? Sacrificed, to be sure, to partisan advantage. Elevated into a doctrine, his work collapses. Properly researched, Marx's work would rise again. Let us forget a hundred years of history, a century of prevarication, of intellectual fastidiousness, a century which would have chained reason to impossibility. Let us get back to the thing itself and discover Marx *contra* his interpreters: *habent sua fata libelli.*

Specialists in the history of ideas would doubtless observe that Marx and Engels were stamped by tradition and influenced by the spirit of the age. The definitions in this *Conceptual Concordance* express their conception of the world and history. These definitions were not an attempt at an exhaustive treatment of the whole of reality, yet are more than the testament of two great nineteenth-century thinkers. We must take these definitions in a sense appropriate to the historical context. Engels himself warned us about definitions which are divorced from their proper historical dimension:

> [Certain remarks] rest upon the false assumption that Marx wishes to define where he only investigates, and that in general one might expect fixed, cut-to-measure, once and for all applicable definitions in Marx's works. It is self-evident that where things and their inter-relations are conceived, not as fixed, but as changing, their mental images, the ideas, are likewise subject to change and transformation; and they are not encapsulated in rigid definitions, but are developed in their historical or logical process of formation (*Capital* III, 13–14).

The labour which went into this *Conceptual Concordance* is sadly no guarantee against omissions: *haec facere nec illa omittere.* We are all too conscious of the limits of the finished product compared with the scope of the original plan. We should like to thank in advance any readers who can advise us of unintended lacunae and offer improvements. We hope that the present *Concordance* will promote debate, controversy, criticism, and a better insight, if not into an *oeuvre* worthy of interest, at least into a world-view which has impressed itself on our time.

GÉRARD BEKERMAN

TABLE OF ENTRIES

ABBREVIATIONS AND BIBLIOGRAPHY

Anti-Dühring Frederick Engels, *Anti-Dühring*. London: Lawrence & Wishart 1969 (first published 1877–8).

Capital Karl Marx, *Capital* 3 Vols. (Vol. 1: trans. Samuel Moore and Edward Aveling, ed. Frederick Engels. London: Lawrence & Wishart 1977 (first published 1867). Vol. 2: ed. Frederick Engels. London: Lawrence & Wishart 1970 (written 1867–79). Vol. 3. ed. Frederick Engels. London: Lawrence & Wishart 1972 (written 1864–5).

Contribution to Critique of Political Economy Karl Marx, *A Contribution to the Critique of Political Economy*, trans. S. W. Ryazanskaya, ed. Maurice Dobb. London: Lawrence & Wishart 1971 (first published 1859).

CW Karl Marx and Frederick Engels, *Collected Works*. London: Lawrence & Wishart 1975 etc. (Short titles and original dates follow each reference).

Dialectics of Nature Frederick Engels, *Dialectics of Nature*, trans. Clemens Dutt. London: Lawrence & Wishart 1954 (written 1873–86).

E Indicates a text written by Frederick Engels. (All other texts were written by Karl Marx or jointly written by Marx and Engels.)

First International Karl Marx, *The First International and After*, ed. David Fernbach. Harmondsworth and London: Penguin/New Left Review 1974. (Short titles and original dates follow each reference.)

Grundrisse Karl Marx, *Grundrisse der Kritik der politischen Ökonomie*, Europäische Verlagsanstalt/Europa Verlag, Frankfurt/Vienna, n.d. (Translations from manuscripts included in this collection, but excluded from the Penguin *Grundrisse*, are my own.)

Paris Commune   Karl Marx and Friedrich Engels, *Writings on the Paris Commune*, ed. Hal Draper. New York and London: Monthly Review Press 1971. (Short titles and original dates follow each reference.)

Penguin *Capital*   Karl Marx, *Capital* 3 Vols. (Vol. 1: trans. Ben Fowkes. Harmondsworth and London: Penguin/New Left Review 1976. Cited for comparison with *Capital* 1 translations, except for passages from an appendix, 'Results of the Immediate Process of Production', pp. 948–1084, trans. Rodney Livingstone (written 1863–6). Vol. 2: trans. David Fernbach. Harmondsworth and London: Penguin/New Left Review 1978. Cited for comparison with *Capital* 2 translations. Vol. 3: trans. David Fernbach. Harmondsworth and London: Penguin/New Left Review 1981. Cited for comparison with *Capital* 3 translations.)

Penguin *Grundrisse*   Karl Marx, *Grundrisse*, trans. Martin Nicolaus. Harmondsworth and London: Penguin/New Left Review 1974 (written 1857–9).

SC   Karl Marx and Frederick Engels, *Selected Correspondence*, 2nd. edn, trans. I. Lasker, ed. S. Ryazanskaya. Moscow: Progress Publishers 1965. (Recipients and dates cited for each reference.)

SW   Karl Marx and Frederick Engels, *Selected Works in one Volume*. London: Lawrence & Wishart 1973. (Short titles and original dates follow each reference.)

SW 1 or 2   Karl Marx and Frederick Engels, *Selected Works in two volumes*. Moscow: Foreign Languages Publishing House 1962. (Short

titles and original dates follow each reference.)

Texts on Method   Karl Marx, *Texts on Method*, trans. and ed.
Terrell Carver. Oxford: Basil Blackwell;
New York: Barnes & Noble 1975. (Short
titles and original dates follow each reference.)

Theories of Surplus Value Karl Marx, *Theories of Surplus Value* 3 Vols.
(Vol. 1: trans. Émile Burns, ed. S. Ryazan-
skaya. London: Lawrence & Wishart 1969
(written 1862–3). Vol. 2: trans. Renate
Simpson. Lawrence & Wishart 1969
(written 1862–3). Vol. 3: trans. Jack
Cohen, ed. S. Ryazanskaya and Richard
Dixon. Lawrence and Wishart 1972
(written 1862–3).

Werke   Karl Marx and Friedrich Engels, *Werke*.
Berlin: Dietz Verlag 1956 etc. (My own
translations from material otherwise
unavailable in English. Short titles and
original dates follow each reference.)

A

Abstraction   *See* Labour.

Abundance

Includes both mass and variety of use-values, and in turn implies a profuse development of man as producer, an all-round development of his productive capacities (*Theories of Surplus Value* 3.55).
See also Labour.

Accessory (in production)

Raw material may either form the principal substance of a product, or it may enter into its formation only as an accessory. An accessory may be consumed by the instruments of labour, as coal under a boiler (*Capital* 1.177; Penguin *Capital* 1.288).
See also Production.

Accounting   *See* Cost of circulation.

Accumulation

A process which takes place in time (Penguin *Grundrisse* 231).
Conquest of the world of social wealth (*Capital* 1.555; Penguin *Capital* 1.739).
But, so far as he [the capitalist] is personified capital, it is not values in use and the enjoyment of them, but exchange-value and its augmentation, that spur him into action. Fanatically bent on making value expand itself, he ruthlessly forces the human race to produce for production's sake; he thus forces the development of the productive powers of society, and creates those material conditions, which alone can form the

real basis of a higher form of society, a society in which the full and free development of every individual forms the ruling principle. . . . Accumulate, accumulate! That is Moses and the prophets! (*Capital* 1.555,558; Penguin *Capital* 1.739,742).

Capitalization of surplus-value (*Capital* 2.323; Penguin *Capital* 2.394).

Conversion of surplus-value into productive capital (*Capital* 2.335; Penguin *Capital* 2.405).

A process of reproduction on a progressively increasing scale (*Capital* 2.324; Penguin *Capital* 2.395).

Expansion of production (*Capital* 2.493; Penguin *Capital* 2.565).

Snatching of surplus-value and its capitalization (*Capital* 2.507; Penguin *Capital* 2.579).

A material means of increasing productiveness (*Capital* 3.218; Penguin *Capital* 3.324).

See also Foreign trade.

accumulation (actual)

The transformation of the value of commodity-capital, etc., into money (*Capital* 3.509; Penguin *Capital* 3.641).

accumulation fund

[It] can be invested by the person controlling it as new fixed capital (or also circulating capital) (*Theories of Surplus Value* 2.480).

See also Insurance fund; Money-accumulation fund.

accumulation of capital

The separation and the independent existence of material wealth as against labour on an ever increasing scale (*Theories of Surplus Value* 3.315).

As simple reproduction constantly reproduces the capital-relation itself, i.e. the relation of capitalists on the one hand, and wage-workers on the other, so reproduction on a progressive scale, i.e. accumulation, reproduces the capital-relation on a progressive scale, more capitalists or larger capitalists at this pole, more wage-workers at that. . . . Accumulation of capital is, therefore, increase of the proletariat (*Capital* 1.575–6; Penguin *Capital* 1.763–4).

The gradual increase of capital by reproduction as it passes from the circular to the spiral form (*Capital* 1.588; Penguin *Capital* 1.780).

accumulation of loan capital

The accumulation of loan capital consists simply in the fact that money is precipitated as loanable money. This process is very different from an actual transformation into capital; it is merely the accumulation of money in a form in which it can be transformed into capital. . . . [It] expresses . . . the extent of the transformation of the industrial capitalists into mere money-capitalists (*Capital* 3.507; Penguin *Capital* 3.639).

accumulation process

One facet of the capitalist production process (*Capital* 3.219; Penguin *Capital* 3.325).

capitalist accumulation *See* Law.

primitive accumulation

Historical process of divorcing the producer from the means of production (*Capital* 1.668; Penguin *Capital* 1.874–5).

The spoliation of the church's property, the fraudulent alienation of the State domains, the robbery of the common lands, the usurpation of feudal and clan property, and its transformation into modern private property under circumstances of reckless terrorism, were just so many idyllic methods of primitive accumulation (*Capital* 1.685; Penguin *Capital* 1.895).

The discovery of gold and silver in America, the extirpation, enslavement and entombment in mines of the aboriginal population, the beginning of the conquest and looting of the East Indies, the turning of Africa into a warren for the commercial hunting of black-skins, signalised the rosy dawn of the era of capitalist production. These idyllic proceedings are the chief momenta of primitive accumulation (*Capital* 1.703; Penguin *Capital* 1.915).

Expropriation of the immediate producers, i.e. the dissolution of private property based on the labour of its owner (*Capital* 1.713; Penguin *Capital* 1.927).

The separation of labour and the worker from the conditions of labour, which confront him as independent forces (*Theories of Surplus Value* 3.271).

3

The conditions of labour acquire an independent existence in relation to the worker and to labour itself (*Theories of Surplus Value* 3.314–15).
See also Workhouses.

Act of production

Repeated labour-processes (*Capital* 2.232; Penguin *Capital* 2.306).

duration of the productive act

Duration of the productive act, i.e. the duration of the repeated labour-processes required to get out a finished product, to market it as a commodity, hence to convert it from productive into commodity capital (*Capital* 2.232; Penguin *Capital* 2.306).

Agricultural proletariat   *See* Proletariat.

Agriculture

The primary branch of production (*Theories of Surplus Value* 1.46).
A particular field of exploitation for capital (*Capital* 3.618; Penguin *Capital* 3.755).
Investment for capital in a particular sphere of production (*Capital* 3.618; Penguin *Capital* 3.755).
Pure production of raw products (*Theories of Surplus Value* 2.81).
See also Rent.

Alienation

Relationship in which man stands to himself (*CW* 3.277; [*Economic and Philosophical Manuscripts*, written 1844]).
Fact of political economy (*CW* 3.278 [*Economic and Philosophical Manuscripts*, written 1844]).
Estrangement is manifested not only in the fact that my means of life belong to someone else, that which I desire is the inaccessible possession of another, but also in the fact that every-

thing is itself something different from itself – that my activity is something else and that, finally (and this applies also to the capitalist), all is under [the sway] of inhuman power (*CW* 3.314 [*Economic and Philosophical Manuscripts*, written 1844]).

The propertied class and the class of the proletariat present the same human self-estrangement. But the former class feels at ease and strengthened in this self-estrangement, it recognizes estrangement as its own power and has in it the semblance of a human existence (*CW* 4.36 [*Holy Family*, first published 1845]).

See also Accumulation, primitive; Capital; Communism; Division of labour; Supersession; Wealth.

Relating of labour to its objective conditions – and hence to the objectivity created by itself – as alien property (Penguin *Grundrisse* 515).

See also Labour.

Man's realization is his loss of reality, it is an alien reality (*CW* 3.299 [*Economic and Philosophical Manuscripts*, written 1844]).

A commodity can only be alienated in exchange for another commodity, or if we regard the matter from the standpoint of the owner of the other commodity, he too can only alienate, i.e. realize, his commodity by bringing it into contact with the particular need of which it is the object (*Contribution to Critique of Political Economy* 43).

Selling [*Veräusserung*] is the practical aspect of alienation [*Entäusserung*] (*CW* 3.174 [*On the Jewish Question*, first published 1844]).

Anarchy

The law of civil society emancipated from divisive privileges (*CW* 4.117 [*Holy Family*, first published 1845]).

Anthropology   *See* Freedom; Labour; Life; Man; Nature; Species-being.

Anti-semitism

Mark of a backward culture (*Werke* 22.49 [*Über den Anti-semitismus*, first published 1890 E]).

5

The reaction of the medieval, declining strata of society against the modern social order, which consists essentially of capitalists and wage-labourers (*Werke* 22.50 [*Über den Antisemitismus*, first published 1890 E]).

Sub-species of feudal socialism (*Werke* 22.50 [*Über den Antisemitismus*, first published 1890 E]).

If I had to choose, then better Jewish than titled! (*Werke* 22.51 [*Über den Antisemitismus*, first published 1890 E]).

Approvisionnement

Money expressed in the form of articles of consumption, use-values, which the worker obtains from the capitalist in the act of exchange between the two of them (Penguin *Grundrisse* 300).

The part of capital entering into small-scale circulation (Penguin *Grundrisse* 678).

Arithmetic (political)

The first form in which political economy is treated as a separate science (*Contribution to Critique of Political Economy* 53–4).

Average

An external abstraction (Penguin *Grundrisse* 137).

The moving principle of the oscillations which commodity prices run through during a given epoch (Penguin *Grundrisse* 137).

Average labour   *See* Labour; Value.

Average price   *See* Price.

Average profit   *See* Profit.

B

Balance of payments

The balance of payments differs from the balance of trade in that it is a balance of trade which must be settled at a definite time (*Capital* 3.517; Penguin *Capital* 3.649).

Bank   *See* Credit.

central bank

Pivot of the credit system (*Capital* 3.572; Penguin *Capital* 3.706).
See also Production.

Bank capital   *See* Capital.

Banker(s)

Money-lenders by profession (*Capital* 3.478; Penguin *Capital* 3.609).

Banking system

The banking system, so far as its formal organization and centralization is concerned, is the most artificial and most developed product turned out by the capitalist mode of production (*Capital* 3.606; Penguin *Capital* 3.742).

Bank note

A draft upon a banker, payable at any time to the bearer, and given by the banker in place of private drafts (*Capital* 3.403; Penguin *Capital* 3.529).

7

Circulating token of credit (*Capital* 3.404; Penguin *Capital* 3.529).

Barter

The spontaneous form of exchange (*Contribution to Critique of Political Economy* 50).
See also Merchant Capital; Commercial capital.

Base   *See* State; Structure (economic).

economic base *See* Economy; History; Relations; Society; State; Structure (economic).

Being

An open question beyond the point where our sphere of observation ends (*Anti-Dühring* 58 E).
See also Consciousness; Essence; Man.

Bills of exchange

Actual commercial money (*Capital* 3.400; Penguin *Capital* 3.525).
Real foundation of credit (*Capital* 3.400; Penguin *Capital* 3.525).
Instrument of circulation (*Capital* 3.400; Penguin *Capital* 3.525).

Bonapartism

Bonapartism is the necessary form of government in a country where the working class – highly developed in the towns but outnumbered by the small peasants on the land – has been defeated in a great revolutionary struggle by the capitalist class, the petty bourgeoisie and the army (*First International* 138–9 [*Prussian Military Question*, first published 1865 E]).
The real religion of the modern bourgeoisie (*SC* 177 [to Marx, 13 April 1866 E]).

Bourgeois

Slave of social conditions and the prejudices involved in them (*CW* 4.528 [*Condition of the Working Class*, first published 1845 E]).
See also Credit; State; Stock exchange.

Bourgeoisie

Bourgeois class (*CW* 6.342 [*Principles of Communism*, written 1847 E]).
Class of big capitalists who already in all civilized countries almost exclusively own all the means of subsistence and the raw materials and instruments (machinery, factories, etc.), needed for the production of these means of subsistence (*CW* 6.342 [*Principles of Communism*, written 1847 E]).
Class of modern capitalists, owners of the means of social production and employers of wage-labour (*CW* 6.482 [*Communist Manifesto*, footnote first published 1888 E]).
Defenders of property (*CW* 12.221 [*British Rule in India*, first published 1853]).
Exploiting and oppressing class (*SW* 1.24 [Preface to *Communist Manifesto*, first published 1883 E]).
See also Bonapartism; Fraternity; Free trade; Growth (of productive capital); Revolution; Workhouses.

Bullion reserves

The determination of the metal reserve of the so called national banks, a determination, however, which does not by itself regulate the magnitude of this metal hoard, for it can grow solely by the paralysis of domestic and foreign trade, is three-fold: (1) reserve fund for international payments, in other words, reserve fund of world-money; (2) reserve fund for alternatively expanding and contracting domestic metal circulation; (3) reserve fund for the payment of deposits and for the convertibility of notes (*Capital* 3.567–8; Penguin *Capital* 3.701).
See also Savings banks.

Bureaucracy

The 'bureaucracy' is the 'state formalism' of civil society. It is the 'state consciousness', the 'state will', the 'state power', as one corporation – and thus a particular, closed society within the state. (The 'general interest' can maintain itself against the particular as 'something particular' only so long as the particular maintains itself against the general as 'something general'. The bureaucracy must therefore protect the imaginary generality of the particular interest, the spirit of the corporations, in order to protect the imaginary particularity of the general interest – its own spirit). . . . A particular, closed society in the state [*Werke* 1.248]. . . . The bureaucratic spirit is a jesuitical, theological spirit through and through. The bureaucrats are the jesuits and theologians of the state. The bureaucracy is *la république prêtre*. . . . The bureaucracy has the state, the spiritual essence of society, in its possession, as its private property. The general spirit of the bureaucracy is the secret, the mystery, preserved within itself by the hierarchy and against the outside world by being a closed corporation. . . . Hence, authority is the basis of its knowledge, and the deification of authority is its conviction. . . . The state only continues to exist as various fixed bureaucratic minds, bound together in subordination and passive obedience (*CW* 3.45–7 [*Critique of Hegel's Philosophy of Law*, written 1843]).

Business hours

Time of purchase and sale (*Capital* 2.132; Penguin *Capital* 2.207).
See also Cost of circulation.

C

Capacity for labour

Use-value whose consumption coincides with the objectification of labour and the fixing of exchange value (*Grundrisse* 944).

The commodity belonging to the workers (*Theories of Surplus Value* 1.45).

Subjective condition of labour (Penguin *Capital* 1.981).

The immediate existence of human activity as activity (*CW* 4.49 [*Holy Family*, first published 1845]).

Quantitative form of existence of labour (*Contribution to Critique of Political Economy* 29).

Capital

Accumulated labour (*CW* 3.237 [*Economic and Philosophical Manuscripts*, written 1844]).

Governing power over labour and its products (*CW* 3.247 [*Economic and Philosophical Manuscripts*, written 1844]).

Stored-up labour (*CW* 3.247 [*Economic and Philosophical Manuscripts*, written 1844]).

Very practical, very objective products of workers' self-estrangement (*CW* 4.53 [*Holy Family*, first published 1845]).

A social relation of production (*CW* 9.212 [*Wage Labour and Capital*, first published 1849]).

A production relation of bourgeois society (*CW* 9.212 [*Wage Labour and Capital*, first published 1849]).

Sum of commodities, of exchange values, of social magnitudes (*CW* 9.212 [*Wage Labour and Capital*, first published 1849]).

Industrial power (*CW* 8.232 [*Magyar Struggle*, first published 1849 E]).

That kind of property which exploits wage-labour, and which cannot increase except upon condition of begetting a new

11

supply of wage-labour for fresh exploitation (*CW* 6.498 [*Communist Manifesto*, first published 1848]).

The economic power of bourgeois society, the power ruling over everything (*Texts on Method* 81 [*Introduction to the Grundrisse*, written 1857]).

Not a simple relation, but a process, in whose various moments it is always capital (Penguin *Grundrisse* 258).

Negated individualized labour (Penguin *Grundrisse* 471).

The existence of social labour – the combination of labour as subject as well as object – but this existence as itself existing independently opposite its real moments – hence itself a particular existence apart from them (Penguin *Grundrisse* 471).

It is posited within the concept of capital that the objective conditions of labour – and these are its own product – take on a personality towards it, or, what is the same, that they are posited as the property of a personality alien to the worker. The concept of capital contains the capitalist. Still, this error is in no way greater than that of e.g. all philologists who speak of capital in antiquity, of Roman, Greek capitalists. This is only another way of expressing that labour in Rome and Greece was free, which these gentlemen would hardly wish to assert. The fact that we now not only call the plantation owners in America capitalists, but that they are capitalists, is based on their existence as anomalies within a world market based on free labour. If the concern is the word, capital, which does not occur in antiquity then the still migrating hordes with their herds on the Asiatic high plateau are the biggest capitalists, since capital originally means cattle, which is why the *métairie* contact still frequently drawn up in southern France, for lack of capital, just as an exception, is called: *Bail de bestes à cheptel.* If one wants to descend to bad Latin, then our capitalists or *Capitales Homines* would be those '*qui debent censum de capite*'. The conceptual specification of capital encounters difficulties which do not occur with money; capital is essentially capitalist (Penguin *Grundrisse* 512–13).

Capital itself is the moving contradiction, [in] that it presses to reduce labour-time to a minimum, while it posits labour-time, on the other side, as sole measure and source of wealth (Penguin *Grundrisse* 706).

Combined labour, just as it is in and for itself already a social, combined force (Penguin *Grundrisse* 529).

Necessary form into which exchange-value-creating labour – production founded on exchange-value – must flow (*Grundrisse* 946).

A live monster that is fruitful and multiplies (*Capital* 1.189; Penguin *Capital* 1.302).

A coercive relation, which compels the working-class to do more work than the narrow round of its own life-wants prescribes (*Capital* 1.293; Penguin *Capital* 1.424–5).

Dead labour, that, vampire-like, only lives by sucking living labour, and lives the more, the more labour it sucks (*Capital* 1.224; Penguin *Capital* 1.342).

Command over unpaid labour (*Capital* 1.500; Penguin *Capital* 1.672).

Self-expanding value (*Capital* 1.531; Penguin *Capital* 1.711).

A movement, a circuit-describing process going through various stages, which itself comprises three different forms of the circuit-describing process. Therefore it can be understood only as motion, not as a thing at rest (*Capital* 2.108; Penguin *Capital* 2.185).

Alienated, independent, social power (*Capital* 3.264; Penguin *Capital* 3.373).

Capital is not a thing, but rather a definite social production relation, belonging to a definite historical formation of society, which is manifested in a thing and lends this thing a specific social character. Capital is not the sum of the material and produced means of production; capital is rather the means of production transformed into capital, which in themselves are no more capital than gold or silver in itself is money. It is the means of production monopolized by a certain section of society, confronting living labour-power as products and working conditions rendered independent of this very labour-power, which are personified through this antithesis in capital. It is not merely the products of labourers turned into independent powers, products as rulers and buyers of their producers, but rather also the social forces and the future . . . form of this labour, which confront the labourers as properties of their products. Here then we have a definite and, at first glance, very mystical, social form, of one of the factors in a historically produced social production process (*Capital* 3.814–15; Penguin *Capital* 3.953–4).

The means of enslaving and exploiting labour (*SW* 290 [*Civil War in France*, first published 1871]).

See also Accumulation, of capital; Credit-capital; Means of production; Merchant capital; Money-capital; Money-dealing capital; Social capital.

advanced constant capital

The capital-values advanced for production in the form of both means of production and means of subsistence (*Capital* 2.229; Penguin *Capital* 2.303).

bank capital

Bank capital consists of (1) cash money, gold or notes; (2) securities. The latter can be subdivided into two parts: commercial paper or bills of exchange, which run for a period, become due from time to time, and whose discounting constitutes the essential business of the banker; and public securities, such as government bonds, treasury notes, stocks of all kinds, in short, interest-bearing paper which is however significantly different from bills of exchange. Mortgages may also be included here. The capital composed of these tangible component parts can again be divided into the banker's invested capital and into deposits, which constitute his banking capital, or borrowed capital. In the case of banks which issue notes, these must also be included. We shall leave the deposits and notes out of consideration for the present. It is evident at any rate that the actual component parts of the banker's capital (money, bills of exchange, deposit currency) remain unaffected whether the various elements represent the banker's own capital or deposits, i.e. the capital of other people (*Capital* 3.463–4; Penguin *Capital* 3.594–5).

capital and revenue

As the variable capital always stays in the hands of the capitalist in some form or other, it cannot be claimed in any way that it converts itself into revenue for anyone (*Capital* 2.452; Penguin *Capital* 2.523).

capital in land

Capital incorporated in the land (*Capital* 3.618; Penguin *Capital* 3.756).

capital of circulation

Commodity-capital and money-capital (*Capital* 2.200; Penguin *Capital* 2.275).

circulating and fixed capital

The definiteness of form of fixed and circulating capital arises merely from the different turnovers of the capital-value, functioning in the process of production, or of the *productive capital*. This difference in turnover arises in its turn from the different manner in which the various components of productive capital transfer their value to the product; it is not due to the different parts played by these components in the generation of product value, nor to their characteristic behaviour in the process of self-expansion. Finally the difference in the delivery of value to the product – and therefore the different manner in which this value is circulated by the product and is renewed in its original bodily form through the metamorphoses of the product – arises from the difference of the material shapes in which the productive capital exists, one portion of it being entirely consumed during the creation of an individual product and the other being used up only gradually. Hence it is only the productive capital which can be divided into fixed and circulating capital. But this antithesis does not apply to the other two modes of existence of industrial capital, that is to say, commodity-capital and money-capital, nor does it exist as an antithesis of these two modes to productive capital. It exists *only for productive capital and within its sphere.* No matter how much money-capital and commodity-capital may function as capital and no matter how fluently they may circulate, they cannot become circulating capital as distinct from fixed capital until they are transformed into circulating components of productive capital. But because these two forms of capital dwell in the sphere of circulation, political economy . . . has been misled since the time of Adam Smith into lumping them together with the circulating part of productive capital and assigning them to the category of circulating capital. They are indeed circulation capital in contrast to productive capital, but they are not circulating capital in contrast to fixed capital (*Capital* 2.170–1; Penguin *Capital* 2.246–7).

In addition to the distinction between constant and variable capital, which arises from the immediate process of production in which the capital is involved, there is also a distinction between fixed and circulating capital, which arises from the process of the circulation of capital (*SC* 132 [to Engels, 2 August 1862]).

See also Crises, commercial.

circulating capital

Fluid capital (*Capital* 2.161; Penguin *Capital* 2.238).

Not only wages but also raw materials and auxiliary materials (*Theories of Surplus Value* 2.132).

circulating constant capital

The money into which the commodity is reconverted is in part transformed into a productive supply (*Capital* 2.298; Penguin *Capital* 2.370).

circulating variable capital

Portion of the money realized by the sale of the commodity held in the form of a money-supply in order to be gradually expended in payment of the labour-power incorporated in the process of production (*Capital* 2.298; Penguin *Capital* 2.370).

composition of capital   *See* Composition.

constant capital

That part of capital then, which is represented by the means of production, by the raw material, auxiliary material and the instruments of labour, does not, in the process of production, undergo any quantitative alteration of value (*Capital* 1.202; Penguin *Capital* 1.317).

The labour materialized in the conditions of labour – materials and means of labour (*Theories of Surplus Value* 3.327).

The variable capital is resolved into revenue, firstly wages, secondly profit. If therefore capital is conceived as something contrasted with revenue, the constant capital appears to be capital in the strict sense; the part of the total product that belongs to production and enters into the costs of production without being individually consumed by anyone. This part may originate entirely from profit and wages. In the last analysis, it can never originate from these alone; it is the product of labour, but of labour which regarded the instrument of production itself as revenue. (*Theories of Surplus Value* 1.219). *See also* Instrument and material of labour.

constant and variable capital

I must here remind the reader that the categories, 'variable and constant capital' were first used by me. Political economy since the time of Adam Smith has confusedly mixed up the essential distinctions involved in these categories, with the mere formal differences, arising out of the process of circulation, of fixed and circulating capital (*Capital* 1.572; Penguin *Capital* 1.760).

essence of capital

The relationship between labour and capital (*CW* 4.52 [*Holy Family*, first published 1845]).

estate capital

Capital in these towns [of the middle ages] was a naturally evolved capital, consisting of a house, the tools of the craft, and the natural, hereditary customers; and not being realizable, on account of the backwardness of intercourse and the lack of circulation, it had to be handed down from father to son. Unlike modern capital, which can be assessed in money and which may be indifferently invested in this thing or that, this capital was directly connected with the particular work of the owner, inseparable from it and to this extent estate capital (*CW* 5.66 [*German Ideology*, written 1845–6]).

fallow capital

That part of the latent productive capital which is held in readiness only as a requisite for the productive process, such as cotton, coal, etc. in a spinning-mill, acts as a creator of neither products nor value (*Capital* 2.125; Penguin *Capital* 2.201).

17

fictitious capital

Illusory capital (*Capital* 3.465; Penguin *Capital* 3.595).
See also Interest; Capitalization.

fixed capital

An animated monster (Penguin *Grundrisse* 470).
An element in the money-reserve fund (*Capital* 2.175; Penguin *Capital* 2.251).
Fixed capital is a source of value only in so far as it is itself objectified labour-time, and in so far as it posits surplus labour-time (Penguin *Grundrisse* 702).
Capital is not called fixed because it is fixed in the instruments of labour but because a part of its value laid out in instruments of labour remains fixed in them, while the other part circulates as a component part of the value of the product (*Capital* 2.202; Penguin *Capital* 2.276).
See also Instrument and material of labour.

industrial capital

Accomplished objective form of private property (*CW* 3.293 [*Economic and Philosophical Manuscripts*, written 1844]).
The two forms assumed by capital-value at the various stages of its circulation are those of money-capital and commodity-capital. The form pertaining to the stage of production is that of productive capital. The capital which assumes these forms in the course of its total circuit and then discards them and in each of them performs the function corresponding to the particular form, is industrial capital (*Capital* 2.50; Penguin *Capital* 2.133).
Industrial in the sense that it comprises every branch of industry run on a capitalist basis (*Capital* 2.50; Penguin *Capital* 2.133).
Industrial capital is the only mode of existence of capital in which not only the appropriation of surplus-value, or surplus-product, but simultaneously its creation is a function of capital. Therefore with it the capitalist character of production is a necessity. Its existence implies the class antagonism between capitalists and wage-labourers (*Capital* 2.57; Penguin *Capital* 2.135–6).
See also Circulation-time; Merchant capital; Commodity-capital; Usury.

interest-bearing capital

An essential element of the capitalist mode of production (*Capital* 3.600; Penguin *Capital* 3.735).

Basis of the credit system (*Capital* 3.607; Penguin *Capital* 3.743).

Of all these forms the most complete fetish is interest-bearing capital (*Theories of Surplus Value* 3.453).

Capital as property as distinct from capital as a function (*Capital* 3.379; Penguin *Capital* 3.503).

See also Usury.

latent capital

Fallow capital.

A requisite for the productive process.

Storage of the productive supply.

Component parts of the advanced productive capital.

Instruments of labour whose functioning is interrupted only by the regular pauses of the productive process.

Stage preliminary to the actual productive process (*Capital* 2.125–7; Penguin *Capital* 2.201–2).

The term 'latent' is borrowed from the idea of latent heat in physics, which has now been almost replaced by the theory of the transformation of energy. Marx therefore uses in the third part (a later version), another term, borrowed from the idea of potential energy, viz: 'potential' or analogous to the virtual velocities of D'Alembert, 'virtual capital' (*Capital* 2.80 E; Penguin *Capital* 2.158 E).

loan capital   *See* Accumulation, of loan capital; Shares.

mercantile capital

The mediator between production (industrial capital) and circulation (the consuming public) or between exchange-value and use-value (Penguin *Grundrisse* 332).

minimum of variable capital

Cost-price of a single labour-power, employed the whole year through, day in, day out, for the production of surplus-value (*Capital* 1.291; Penguin *Capital* 1.422).

new constant capital
Products exclusively intended to function as means of production in the labour-process and hence as constant capital in
the accompanying process of self-expansion of value (*Capital*
2.430; Penguin *Capital* 2.502).

potential productive capital
A supply (*Capital* 2.248; Penguin *Capital* 2.322).

productive capital
Form of capital-value pertaining to the stage of production
(*Capital* 2.50; Penguin *Capital* 2.133).
Capital employed in the direct process of production (*Theories
of Surplus Value* 1.413).
See also Circuit; Growth; Labour-power; Production-time;
Self-expansion of value.

release of capital
By release of capital we mean that a portion of the total value
of the product which had to be reconverted into constant or
variable capital up to a certain time, becomes disposable and
superfluous, should production continue on the previous scale
(*Capital* 3.111; Penguin *Capital* 3.206).

tie-up of capital
By tie-up of capital we mean that certain portions of the total
value of the product must be reconverted into elements of
constant and variable capital if production is to proceed on
the same scale (*Capital* 3.111; Penguin *Capital* 3.206).

variable capital
That part of capital, represented by labour-power, which
does, in the process of production, undergo an alteration of
value; it both reproduces the equivalent of its own value, and
also produces an excess, a surplus-value (*Capital* 1.202;
Penguin *Capital* 1.317).
The expression in money of the total value of all the labour-
powers that the capitalist employs simultaneously (*Capital*
1.287; Penguin *Capital* 1.417).

Particular historical form of appearance of the fund for providing the necessaries of life, or the labour-fund which the labourer requires for the maintenance of himself and family, and which, whatever the system of social production, he must himself produce and reproduce (*Capital* 1.533; Penguin *Capital* 1.713).
That part of the product of the annual labour which is required for the reproduction of the working class (*Theories of Surplus Value* 2.416).
See also Composition of capital; Instrument and material of labour.

Capitalist

Capital personified and endowed with consciousness and a will.
The rational miser (*Capital* 1.151; Penguin *Capital* 1.254).
Owner of the means of production (*Theories of Surplus Value* 1.408).
Owner of surplus-value (*Capital* 1.555; Penguin *Capital* 1.738).
A fanatic in making value expand itself (*Capital* 1.555; Penguin *Capital* 1.739).
Owner of the means of production (*SW* 427 [*Socialism, Utopian and Scientific*, first published 1880 E]).
An individual element of the capitalist class (*Capital* 2.355; Penguin *Capital* 2.427).
A functionary of capital (*Theories of Surplus Value* 1.170).
Direct exploiter of the workers (*Theories of Surplus Value* 2.328).
Owner of the surplus labour or of the surplus produce (*Theories of Surplus Value* 3.240).
Commodity owner (*Theories of Surplus Value* 3.458).
Manager (*Theories of Surplus Value* 3.495).
Director of labour (*Theories of Surplus Value* 3.496).
We have a mathematically precise proof why capitalists form a veritable freemason society *vis-à-vis* the whole working-class, while there is little love lost between them in competition among themselves (*Capital* 3.198; Penguin *Capital* 3.300).
See also Bonapartism; Bourgeoisie; *Faux frais* (of production); International; Means of consumption; Republic (democratic).

industrial capitalist
Functionary in the process of production (*Theories of Surplus Value* 2.328).
See also Accumulation, of loan capital; Merchant capital; Profit, gross; Supervision.

money-capitalist
Lender (*Capital* 3.374; Penguin *Capital* 3.497).

Capitalization
Formation of a fictitious capital (*Capital* 3.466; Penguin *Capital* 3.597).

Categories
Historical and transitory products (*CW* 6.166 [*Poverty of Philosophy*, first published 1847]).

categories of bourgeois economics
Forms of thought expressing with social validity the conditions and relations of a definite, historically determined mode of production, viz. the production of commodities (*Capital* 1.80; Penguin *Capital* 1.169).

economic categories
Theoretical expressions.
Abstractions of the social relations of production (*CW* 6.165 [*Poverty of Philosophy*, first published 1847]).

Censor
A police executioner who mishandles the product of my mind by applying an external standard alien to the matter in question (*CW* 4.83 [*Holy Family*, first published 1845]).

Censorship
Criticism as a monopoly of the government (*CW* 1.159 [*Freedom of the Press*, first published 1842]).
See also Freedom of the press.

Centralization

Concentration of capitals already formed, destruction of their individual independence, expropriation of capitalist by capitalist, transformation of many small into few large capitals (*Capital* 1.586; Penguin *Capital* 1.777).
This process differs from the former one of splitting-up in this, that it only presupposes a change in the distribution of capital already to hand, and functioning; its field of action is therefore not limited by the absolute growth of social wealth, by the absolute limits of accumulation. Capital grows in one place to a huge mass in a single hand, because it has in another place been lost by many. This is centralization proper, as distinct from accumulation and concentration (*Capital* 1.586; Penguin *Capital* 1.777).
The swallowing up of the small capitalists by the big and their deprivation of capital (*Capital* 3.246; Penguin *Capital* 3.354).
See also Credit; Nationalization.

Chartism

The political expression of public opinion among the workers (*CW* 4.15 [*Holy Family*, first published 1845 E]).
The compact form of the workers' opposition to the bourgeoisie (*CW* 4.517 [*Condition of the Working Class*, first published 1845 E]).

Chartists

The politically active portion of the British working class (*CW* 11.335 [*Chartists*, first published 1852]).

Christian

From the outset, the Christian was the theorizing Jew (*CW* 3.173 [*On the Jewish Question*, first published 1844]).

Christianity

The sublime thought of Judaism (*CW* 3.173 [*On the Jewish Question*, first published 1844]).
The special religion of capital (*Theories of Surplus Value* 3.448).

23

Circuit

The two phases, each inverse to the other, that make up the metamorphosis of a commodity constitute together a circular movement, a circuit: commodity-form, stripping off of this form, and return to the commodity-form (*Capital* 1.113; Penguin *Capital* 1.207).
See Capital; Circulation; Crises; Reproduction process; Turnover.

circuit of money

Return of money to its point of departure (*Capital* 2.346; Penguin *Capital* 2.416).

circuit of money-capital

The most one-sided, and thus the most striking and typical form in which the circuit of industrial capital appears, the capital whose aim and compelling motive – the self-expansion of value, the making of money, and accumulation – is thus conspicuously revealed (*Capital* 2.61; Penguin *Capital* 2.140).

circuit of productive capital

The form in which classical Political Economy examines the circular movement of industrial capital (*Capital* 2.88; Penguin *Capital* 2.166).
Not only production but a periodical reproduction of surplus-value (*Capital* 2.65; Penguin *Capital* 2.144).
See Capital; Circulation; Crises; Reproduction process; Turnover.

Circulation

The exchange of commodities is the process in which the social metabolism, in other words the exchange of particular products of private individuals, simultaneously gives rise to definite social relations of production, into which individuals enter in the course of this metabolism. As they develop, the interrelations of commodities crystallize into distinct aspects of the universal equivalent, and thus the exchange process becomes at the same time the process of formation of money. This process as a whole, which comprises several processes, constitutes circulation (*Contribution to Critique of Political Economy* 51-2).

The positing of prices, the process in which commodities are transformed into prices: their realization as prices (Penguin *Grundrisse* 187).

Completely developed reciprocal movement of exchange-values (Penguin *Grundrisse* 255).

Process of positing exchange-value, sometimes in the role of the commodity, at other times in the role of money (Penguin *Grundrisse* 256).

Circulation is the movement in which the general alienation appears as general appropriation and general appropriation as general alienation. As much, then, as the whole of this movement appears as a social process, and as much as the individual moments of this movement arise from the conscious will and particular purposes of individuals, so much does the totality of the process appear as an objective interrelation, which arises spontaneously from nature; arising, it is true, from the mutual influence of conscious individuals on one another, but neither located in their consciousness, nor subsumed under them as a whole. Their own collisions with one another produce an alien social power standing above them, produce their mutual interaction as a process and power independent of them. Circulation, because a totality of the social process, is also the first form in which the social relation appears as something independent of the individuals, but not only as, say, in a coin or in exchange value, but extending to the whole of the social movement itself. The social relation of individuals to one another as a power over the individuals which has become autonomous, whether conceived as a natural force, as chance or in whatever other form, is a necessary result of the fact that the point of departure is not the free social individual. Circulation as the first totality among the economic categories is well suited to bring this to light (Penguin *Grundrisse* 196-7).

Sum total of all the mutual relations of commodity-owners (*Capital* 1.162; Penguin *Capital* 1.268).

See also Merchant capital.

circulation of capital

The conversion of a sum of money into means of production and labour-power, is the first step taken by the quantum of value that is going to function as capital. This conversion takes place in the market, within the sphere of circulation. The second step, the process of production, is complete so soon as the means of production have been converted into commodities whose value exceeds that of their component parts, and, therefore, contains the capital originally advanced, plus a surplus-value. These commodities must then be thrown into circulation. They must be sold, their value realised in money, this money afresh converted into capital, and so over and over again. This circular movement, in which the same phases are continually gone through in succession, forms the circulation of capital (*Capital* 1.529, Penguin *Capital* 1.709).

large-scale circulation

The entire period from the moment when capital exits from as wages, exchanged for labouring capacity (Penguin *Grundrisse* 673).

The movement of capital outside the production phase, where its time appears in antithesis to labour time, as circulation time (Penguin *Grundrisse* 678).

small-scale circulation

Continuous and constantly proceeds simultaneously with the production process. It is the part of capital which is paid out as wages, exchanged for labouring capacity (Penguin *Grundrisse* 673).

Appears as contract, exchange, form of intercourse; these things are presupposed before the production process can be set going (Penguin *Grundrisse* 678).

Circulating capital   *See under* Capital.

Circulation-capital

Commodity-capital and money-capital (*Capital* 2.200; Penguin *Capital* 2.275).
See also Capital, circulating, fixed; Merchant capital.

Circulation of commodities

Starting-point of capital (*Capital* 1.145; Penguin *Capital* 1.247).

The circuit made by one commodity in the course of its metamorphoses is inextricably mixed up with the circuits of other commodities.
The total of all the different circuits constitutes the circulation of commodities (*Capital* 1.113; Penguin *Capital* 1.207).
See also Commodity.

Circulation of matter (metabolism)

In so far as exchange is a process, by which commodities are transferred from hands in which they are non-use-values, to hands in which they become use-values, it is a social circulation of matter (*Capital* 1.106; Penguin *Capital* 1.198).
See also Circulation; Commodity-capital; Freedom; Labour; Life.

Circulation-time

The time which capital requires for its conversion from commodities into money, and that which it requires for its conversion from money into commodities (*Capital* 2.129; Penguin *Capital* 2.204).
The time of circulation of capital is a necessary segment of its time of reproduction (*Capital* 2.132; Penguin *Capital* 2.207).
Time of devaluation of capital (Penguin *Grundrisse* 538).
Determines value only in so far as it appears as a natural barrier to the realization of labour-time. Or is therefore in fact a deduction from surplus labour-time, i.e. an increase of necessary labour-time (Penguin *Grundrisse* 539).
A barrier to the productivity of labour (Penguin *Grundrisse* 539).
The entire time of turnover of a given capital is equal to the sum of its time of circulation and its time of production (*Capital* 2.156; Penguin *Capital* 2.233).
The period of time from the moment of the advance of capital-value in a definite form to the return of the functioning capital-value in the same form (*Capital* 2.156; Penguin *Capital* 2.233).

City *See* Town.

Class

An oppressed class is the vital condition for every society founded on the antagonism of classes. The emancipation of the oppressed class thus implies necessarily the creation of a new society. For the oppressed class to be able to emancipate itself it is necessary that the productive powers already acquired and the existing social relations should no longer be capable of existing side by side. Of all the instruments of production, the greatest productive power is the revolutionary class itself. . . . Does this mean that after the fall of the old society there will be a new class domination culminating in a new political power? No.

The condition for the emancipation of the working class is the abolition of all classes, just as the condition for the emancipation of the third estate, of the bourgeois order, was the abolition of all estates and all orders.

The working class, in the course of its development, will substitute for the old civil society an association which will exclude classes and their antagonism, and there will be no more political power properly so-called, since political power is precisely the official expression of antagonism in civil society (*CW* 6.211–12 [*Poverty of Philosophy*, first published 1847]).

And now as to myself, no credit is due to me for discovering the existence of classes in modern society or the struggle between them. Long before me bourgeois historians had described the historical development of this class struggle and bourgeois economists the economic anatomy of the classes. What I did that was new was to prove: (1) that the existence of classes is only bound up with particular historical phases in the development of production, (2) that the class struggle necessarily leads to the dictatorship of the proletariat, (3) that this dictatorship itself only constitutes the transition to the abolition of all classes and to a classless society (*SC* 69 [to Weydemeyer, 5 March 1852]).

In so far as millions of families live under economic conditions of existence that separate their mode of life, their interests and their culture from those of the other classes, and put them in hostile opposition to the latter, they form a class. In so far as there is merely a local interconnection among these small-holding peasants, and the identity of their interests begets no community, no national bond and no political organization among them, they do not form a class (*CW* 11.187 [*Eighteenth Brumaire*, first published 1852]).

The owners merely of labour-power, owners of capital, and landowners, whose respective sources of income are wages, profit and ground-rent, in other words, wage-labourers, capitalists and landowners, constitute then three big classes of modern society based upon the capitalist mode of production. . . . The first question to be answered is this: What constitutes a class? – and the reply to this follows naturally from the reply to another question, namely: What makes wage-labourers, capitalists and landlords constitute the three great social classes?

At first glance – the identity of revenues and sources of revenue. There are three great social groups whose members, the individuals forming them, live on wages, profit and ground-rent respectively, on the realisation of their labour-power, their capital, and their landed property.

However, from this standpoint, physicians and officials, e.g., would also constitute two classes, for they belong to two distinct social groups, the members of each of these groups receiving their revenue from one and the same source. The same would also be true of the infinite fragmentation of interest and rank into which the division of social labour splits labourers as well as capitalists and landlords – the latter, e.g., into owners of vineyards, farm owners, owners of forests, mine owners and owners of fisheries (*Capital* 3.885–6; Penguin *Capital* 3.1025–6).

See also Agricultural proletariat; Anti-semitism; Bourgeoisie; Capital; Communism; Cost of production, of labour; Free-trade; Dialectic; Fraternity; Labour; Nationalization; Need; Party; Proletariat; Revolution; Slavery; State; Supervision; Weaving.

capitalist class   *See* Bonapartism; Bourgeoisie; Capitalist; International; Means of consumption; Republic; Supervision; Unproductive costs.

middle class

Shopkeepers, tradesmen, merchants (*SW* 291 [*Civil War in France*, first published 1871]).

modern classes
Landowners, capitalists (industrialists and merchants) and workers (*SC* 483 [to Schmidt, 12 March 1895 E]).

revolutionary classes
Greatest productive power (*CW* 6.211 [*Poverty of Philosophy*, first published 1847]).

working class
Propertyless class (*CW* 4.304 [*Condition of the Working Class*, first published 1845 E]).

The working class is revolutionary or it is nothing (*SC* 165 [to Schweitzer, 13 February 1865]).

From a social point of view the working class, even when not directly engaged in the labour-process, is just as much an appendage of capital as the ordinary instruments of labour (*Capital* 1.538; Penguin *Capital* 1.719).

Basic condition of capitalist production (*Capital* 2.36; Penguin *Capital* 2.119).

See also Agricultural proletariat; Bonapartism; Capital; Communism; Consumption; Cost of production; International; Law; Nationalization; Need; Party; Pauperism; Republic.

Clock

The first automatic machine applied to practical purposes (*SC* 138 [to Engels, 28 January 1863]).
See also Machine.

Commerce

Verkehr, échange, exchange, *Austausch,* etc., all of which are used both for commercial relations and for characteristic features and mutual relations of individuals as such (*CW* 5.231 [*German Ideology*, written 1845–6]).

I am using the word 'commerce' here in its widest sense, as we use *Verkehr* in German (*SC* 36 [to Annenkov, 28 December 1846]).
See also Relations; State.

Commodity

Products which are exchangeable for others (*CW* 9.213 [*Wage Labour and Capital*, first published 1849]).

Every commodity has a twofold aspect – use-value and exchange-value (*Contribution to Critique of Political Economy* 27).

Objectification of social labour (*Contribution to Critique of Political Economy* 29).

The first category in which bourgeois wealth presents itself (Penguin *Grundrisse* 881).

Immediate unities of use-value and exchange-value (Penguin *Capital* 1.979).

The form in which capital re-appears at the end of the process of production (Penguin *Capital* 1.1059).

The foundation and premiss of capitalist production (Penguin *Capital* 1.1059).

The general form of the product (Penguin *Capital* 1.1060).

Elementary form of bourgeois wealth (Penguin *Capital* 1.949).

An intrinsic feature of the capitalist mode of production (Penguin *Capital* 1.1061).

A very queer thing, abounding in metaphysical subtleties and theological niceties (*Capital* 1.76; Penguin *Capital* 1.163).

All commodities are non-use-values for their owners, and use-values for their non-owners (*Capital* 1.89; Penguin *Capital* 1.179).

See also Circulation of commodities; Exchange-value; Fetishism.

metamorphosis of commodities

First metamorphosis: transformation from a commodity into money. . . . Second metamorphosis: retransformation of the latter from money into a commodity (*Capital* 1.111; Penguin *Capital* 1.205).

Commodity-capital

The circulating commodity, the commodity which realizes itself only by taking on the form of another commodity, which steps outside circulation and serves immediate needs (Penguin *Grundrisse* 254).

Form assumed by capital-value in its circulation (*Capital* 2.50; Penguin *Capital* 2.133).

Money-capital and commodity-capital, so far as they function as vehicles of particular branches of business, side by side with industrial capital, are nothing but modes of existence of the different functional forms now assumed, now discarded by industrial capital in the sphere of circulation (*Capital* 2.57; Penguin *Capital* 2.136).

function of commodity-capital

Ultimate reconversion of capital-value into its original money-form (*Capital* 2.43; Penguin *Capital* 2.126–7).
See also Circuit.

Commodity-supply

Isolation and fixation of the commodity-form of the product (*Capital* 2.147; Penguin *Capital* 2.221).

A premiss of commodity-circulation (*Capital* 2.151; Penguin *Capital* 2.225).

Not a prerequisite of uninterrupted sale, but a consequence of the impossibility of selling the goods (*Capital* 2.151; Penguin *Capital* 2.225).

Commune

A working-class government (*SW* 290 [*Civil War in France*, first published 1871]).

The produce of the struggle of the producing against the appropriating class (*SW* 290 [*Civil War in France*, first published 1871]).

Positive form of the revolution against the Empire and the conditions of its existence (*Paris Commune* 146 [first draft, *Civil War in France*, written 1871]).

Reabsorption of the state power by society (*Paris Commune* 152 [first draft, *Civil War in France*, written 1871]).

Communism

Positive transcendence of private property.
Real appropriation of the human essence by and for man.

Complete return of man to himself as a social (i.e. human) being – a return accomplished consciously and embracing the entire wealth of previous development.

Genuine resolution of the conflict between man and nature and between man and man – the true resolution of the strife between existence and essence, between objectification and self-confirmation, between freedom and necessity, between the individual and the species. Communism is the riddle of history solved, and it knows itself to be this solution (*CW* 3.296–7 [*Economic and Philosophical Manuscripts*, written 1844]).

Position as the negation of the negation (*CW* 3.306 [*Economic and Philosophical Manuscripts*, written 1844]).

Actual phase necessary for the next stage of historical development in the process of human emancipation and rehabilitation (*CW* 3.306 [*Economic and Philosophical Manuscripts*, written 1844]).

Necessary form and dynamic principle of the immediate future (*CW* 3.306 [*Economic and Philosophical Manuscripts*, written 1844]).

In order to abolish the idea of private property, the idea of communism is quite sufficient. It takes actual communist action to abolish actual private property (*CW* 3.313 [*Economic and Philosophical Manuscripts*, written 1844]).

Communism differs from all previous movements in that it overturns the basis of all earlier relations of production and intercourse, and for the first time consciously treats all naturally evolved premises as the creations of hitherto existing men, strips them of their natural character and subjugates them to the power of the united individuals. Its organization is, therefore, essentially economic, the material production of the conditions of this unity; it turns existing conditions into conditions of unity. The reality which communism creates is precisely the true basis for rendering it impossible that anything should exist independently of individuals, in so far as reality is nevertheless only a product of the preceding intercourse of individuals (*CW* 5.81 [*German Ideology*, written 1845–6]).

The communists are distinguished from the other working-class parties by this only: (1) In the national struggles of the proletarians of the different countries, they point out and bring to the front the common interests of the entire proletariat, independently of all nationality. (2) In the various stages of development which the struggle of the working class against the bourgeoisie has to pass through, they always and everywhere represent the interests of the movement as a whole.

The communists, therefore, are on the one hand, practically, the most advanced and resolute section of the working-class parties of every country, that section which pushes forward all others; on the other hand, theoretically, they have over the great mass of the proletariat the advantage of clearly understanding the line of march, the conditions, and the ultimate general results of the proletarian movement.

The distinguishing feature of communism is not the abolition of property generally, but the abolition of bourgeois property (*CW* 6.497–8 [*Communist Manifesto*, first published 1848]).

The real movement which abolishes the present state of things (*CW* 5.49 [*German Ideology*, written 1845–6]).

Democratic revolution by force (*SC* 32 [to Communist Committee, 23 October 1846 E]).

Not a doctrine but a movement (*CW* 6.303 [*Communists and Karl Heinzen*, first published 1847 E]).

Doctrine for the conditions for the emancipation of the proletariat (*CW* 6.341 [*Principles of Communism*, written 1847 E]).

The declaration of the permanence of the revolution (*CW* 10.127 [*Class Struggles in France*, first published 1850]).

The class dictatorship of the proletariat is the necessary transit point to the abolition of class distinctions generally, to the abolition of all the relations of production on which they rest, to the abolition of all the social relations that correspond to these relations of production, to the revolutionizing of all the ideas that result from these social relations (*CW* 10.127 [*Class Struggles in France*, first published 1850]).

Insight into the nature, the conditions and the consequent general aims of the struggle waged by the proletariat (*SW* 437; [*History of Communist League*, first published 1885 E]).

The ultimate solution (*SC* 394 [to Laura Lafargue, 2 October 1886 E]).

Communism is not a mere party doctrine of the working class but a theory, the goal of which is freedom for all of society including capitalists (*Werke* 2.641 [Foreword, *Condition of the Working Class*, first published 1892 E].

In a higher phase of communist society, after the enslaving subordination of the individual to the division of labour, and therewith also the antithesis between mental and physical labour, has vanished; after labour has become not only a means of life but life's prime want; after the productive forces have also increased with the all-round development of the individual, and all the springs of co-operative wealth flow more abundantly – only then can the narrow horizon of bourgeois right be crossed in its entirety and society inscribe on its banners: From each according to his ability, to each according to his needs! (*SW* 320–1 [*Critique of the Gotha Programme*, written 1875]).

communism and socialism

By socialists, in 1847, were understood, on the one hand, the adherents of the various Utopian systems: Owenites in England, Fourierists in France, both of them already reduced to the position of mere sects, and gradually dying out; on the other hand, the most multifarious social quacks, who, by all manners of tinkering, professed to redress, without any danger to capital and profit, all sorts of social grievances, in both cases men outside the working-class movement, and looking rather to the 'educated' classes for support. Whatever portion of the working class had become convinced of the insufficiency of mere political revolutions, and had proclaimed the necessity of a total social change, that portion then called itself communist. It was a crude, rough-hewn, purely instinctive sort of communism; still, it touched the cardinal point and was powerful enough amongst the working class to produce the Utopian communism, in France, of Cabet, and in Germany, of Weitling. Thus, socialism was, in 1847, a middle-class movement, communism a working-class movement. (*SW* 1.27–8 [Preface, *Communist Manifesto*, first published 1888 E]).

Communist

Follower of a definite revolutionary party (*CW* 5.57 [*German Ideology*, written 1845–6]).

35

Community of women

A relationship that belongs altogether to bourgeois society and is completely realized today in prostitution. But prostitution is rooted in private property and falls with it (*CW* 6.354 [*Principles of Communism*, written 1847 E]).
See also Family; Women.

Competition

The completest expression of the battle of all against all which rules in modern civil society. This battle, a battle for life, for existence, for everything, in case of need a battle of life and death, is fought not between the different classes of society only, but also between the individual members of these classes (*CW* 4.375; [*Condition of the Working Class*, first published 1845 E]).
The struggle of capital against capital, of labour against labour (*CW* 3.435 [*Outlines*, first published 1844 E]).
The great mainspring which again and again jerks into activity our aging and withering social order, or rather disorder; but with each new exertion it also saps a part of this order's waning strength (*CW* 3.442 [*Outlines*, first published 1844 E]).
Governs the numerical advance of mankind (*CW* 3.442 [*Outlines*, first published 1844 E]).
Appears historically as the dissolution of compulsory guild membership, government regulation, internal tariffs and the like within a country, as the lifting of blockades, prohibitions, protection on the world market – it appears historically, in short, as the negation of the limits and barriers peculiar to the stages of production preceding capital (Penguin *Grundrisse* 649).
The inner nature of capital, its essential character, appearing in and realized as the reciprocal interaction of many capitals with one another, the inner tendency as external necessity (Penguin *Grundrisse* 414).
Essential locomotive force of the bourgeois economy (Penguin *Grundrisse* 552).
The mode generally in which capital secures the victory of its mode of production (Penguin *Grundrisse* 730).

Transfer of capital or withdrawal of capital from one trade to another (*SC* 130 [to Engels, 2 August 1862]).

Movement towards equilibrium (*Capital* 3.366; Penguin *Capital* 3.488).

See also Division of labour, social division and manufacturing. .

free competition

Ultimate, highest and most developed form of existence of private property (*CW* 6.296 [*Communists and Karl Heinzen*, first published 1847 E]).

A state of society in which every one has the right to engage in any branch of industry he likes, and where nothing can hinder him in carrying it on except lack of the necessary capital (*CW* 6.346 E [*Principles of Communism*, written 1847 E]).

The only state of society in which large-scale industry can grow (*CW* 6.346 [*Principles of Communism*, written 1847 E]).

The relation of capital to itself as another capital, i.e. the real conduct of capital as capital (Penguin *Grundrisse* 650).

See also Division of labour; Free-trade.

universal competition

Pure private property, which has cast off all semblance of a communal institution and has shut out the state from any influence on the development of property (*CW* 5.89–90 [*German Ideology*, written 1845–6]).

Composition of capital

Proportion of active and passive components, i.e. of variable and constant capital (*Capital* 3.145; Penguin *Capital* 3.244).

capitals of average composition

Capitals whose composition coincides with the average (*Capital* 3.164; Penguin *Capital* 3.264).

capitals of higher composition

Such capitals as contain a larger percentage of constant and a smaller percentage of variable capital than the average social capital (*Capital* 3.164; Penguin *Capital* 3.264).

capitals of lower composition

Those capitals in which the constant is relatively smaller, and the variable relatively greater than in the average social capital (*Capital* 3.164; Penguin *Capital* 3.264).

organic composition

The composition of capital is to be understood in a two-fold sense. On the side of value, it is determined by the proportion in which it is divided into constant capital or value of the means of production, and variable capital or value of labour-power, the sum total of wages. On the side of material, as it functions in the process of production, all capital is divided into means of production and living labour-power. This latter composition is determined by the relation between the mass of the means of production employed, on the one hand, and the mass of labour necessary for their employment on the other. I call the former the *value-composition*, the latter the *technical composition* of capital. Between the two there is a strict correlation. To express this, I call the value-composition of capital, in so far as it is determined by its technical composition and mirrors the changes of the latter, the *organic composition* of capital. Wherever I refer to the composition of capital, without further qualification, its organic composition is always understood (*Capital* 1.574; Penguin *Capital* 1.762).
See also Rate of profit, equalization of.

technical composition of capital

The real basis of the organic composition of capital (*Capital* 3.145; Penguin *Capital* 3.244).

technological composition of capital

The ratio between living labour or number of workers . . . represented by variable capital and the quantity of the instruments of labour required (*Theories of Surplus Value* 2.455).

Concentration

In objective form, i.e. as concentration in one hand, which here still coincides with accumulation, of the necessaries of life, of raw material and instruments, or, in a word, of money as the general form of wealth (Penguin *Grundrisse* 585).

In subjective form, the accumulation of labour powers and their concentration at a single point under the command of the capitalist (Penguin *Grundrisse* 585).

Another name for reproduction on an extended scale (*Capital* 1.587; Penguin *Capital* 1.779).

concentration of capital

Accumulation of large amounts of capital by the destruction of the smaller capitals (*Theories of Surplus Value* 3.315).

Attraction, decapitalization of the intermediate links between capital and labour (*Theories of Surplus Value* 3.315).

concentration of the means of production

Necessary condition of their co-operation (*Capital* 1.312; Penguin *Capital* 1.447).

See also Accumulation; Centralization; Degree of concentration (of labour).

Concept

The mediating link between form and content (*CW* 1.15 [to his father, 10–11 November 1837]).

Concepts

The results in which the experiences of natural science are summarized (*Anti-Dühring* 20 E).

Concrete

The concrete is concrete, because it is the sum of many determinations, and therefore a unity of diversity. Hence the concrete appears in thinking as a process of summarization, as a result, not as a starting point, although the concrete is the actual starting point and hence also the starting point of perception and conceptualization (*Texts on Method* 72–3 [*Introduction to the Grundrisse*, written 1857]).

39

Conditions

material conditions
Bearers of definite social relations (*Capital* 3.819; Penguin *Capital* 3.957).

On the one hand prerequisites, on the other hand results and creations of the capitalist process of production (*Capital* 3.819; Penguin *Capital* 3.957).

See also Natural elements; Physical conditions.

Conditions of labour

material conditions of labour
Produced means of production, instruments, raw materials, the land (*Capital* 3.824–5; Penguin *Capital* 3.963–4).

Someone else's property confronting the labourer (*Theories of Surplus Value* 3.460).

objective conditions of labour See Means of production.

subjective conditions of labour See Capacity for labour.

Consciousness
My general consciousness is only the theoretical shape of that of which the living shape is the real community, the social fabric, although at the present day general consciousness is an abstraction from real life and as such confronts it with hostility. The activity of my general consciousness, as an activity, is therefore also my theoretical existence as a social being (*CW* 3.298–9 [*Economic and Philosophical Manuscripts*, written 1844]).

Consciousness can never be anything else than conscious being, and the being of men is their actual life-process (*CW* 5.36 [*German Ideology*, written 1845–6]).

Consciousness is, therefore, from the very beginning a social product, and remains so as long as men exist at all (*CW* 5.44 [*German Ideology*, written 1845–6]).

Consciousness is at first, of course, merely consciousness concerning the immediate sensuous environment and conscious-

ness of the limited connection with other persons and things outside the individual who is growing self-conscious. At the same time it is consciousness of nature, which first confronts men as a completely alien, all-powerful and unassailable force, with which men's relations are purely animal and by which they are overawed like beasts (*CW* 5.44 [*German Ideology*, written 1845–6]).
The mode of production of material life conditions the general process of social, political and intellectual life. It is not the consciousness of men that determines their existence, but their social existence that determines their consciousness (*Contribution to Critique of Political Economy* 20–1).
See also Capital; Equality; Language; Proletariat; Structure (economic).

Consumption

Inner moment of productive activity (*Texts on Method* 64 [*Introduction to the Grundrisse*, written 1857]).
Immediately also production, as in nature the consumption of elements and chemical materials is the production of the plant (*Texts on Method* 59 [*Introduction to the Grundrisse*, written 1857]).
See also Production.

individual consumption

The reconversion of the means of subsistence given by capital in exchange for labour-power, into fresh labour-power at the disposal of capital for exploitation (*Capital* 1.537; Penguin *Capital* 1.718).
Production and reproduction of that means of production so indispensable to the capitalist: the labourer himself (*Capital* 1.537; Penguin *Capital* 1.718).
A mere factor in the process of production (*Capital* 1.538; Penguin *Capital* 1.719).

productive and individual consumption

The labourer consumes in a two-fold way. While producing he consumes by his labour the means of production, and converts them into products with a higher value than that of the capital advanced. This is his productive consumption. It is at the same time consumption of his labour-power by the capitalist who bought it. On the other hand, the labourer turns the money paid to him for his labour-power, into means of subsistence: this is his individual consumption. The labourer's productive consumption, and his individual consumption, are therefore totally distinct. In the former, he acts as the motive power of capital, and belongs to the capitalist. In the latter, he belongs to himself, and performs his necessary vital functions outside the process of production. The result of the one is, that the capitalist lives; of the other, that the labourer lives (*Capital* 1.536; Penguin *Capital* 1.717).

Labour uses up its material factors, its subject and its instruments, consumes them, and is therefore a process of consumption. Such productive consumption is distinguished from individual consumption by this, that the latter uses up products, as means of subsistence for the living individual; the former, as means whereby alone, labour, the labour-power of the living individual, is enabled to act. The product, therefore, of individual consumption, is the consumer himself; the result of productive consumption, is a product distinct from the consumer (*Capital* 1.179; Penguin *Capital* 1.290).

Consumption-fund

Reserve of means of consumption (*Capital* 2.150; Penguin *Capital* 2.224).
See also Wages.

consumption-fund of the capitalists

Surplus-value (*Capital* 1.532; Penguin *Capital* 1.712).

Contingency

Completion and phenomenal form of necessity (*Werke* 39.206 [to Borgius, 25 January 1894 E]).

Contradiction   *See* Capital; Crises; Dialectic; Free trade; Relations of production, bourgeois; Revolution, proletarian.

Cooperation

Numerous labourers working together side by side, whether in one and the same process, or in different but connected processes (*Capital* 1.308; Penguin *Capital* 1.443).
Multiplication of forces (*Werke* 16.212; [review of *Capital*, written 1867 E]).
A specific form of the capitalist process of production (*Capital* 1.317; Penguin *Capital* 1.453).
First change experienced by the actual labour-process when subjected to capital (*Capital* 1.317; Penguin *Capital* 1.453).
See also Centralization; Concentration.

Cost of circulation

The costs of circulation properly . . . are not reducible to productive labour time. But they are also by nature restricted to the time it necessarily costs to transform the commodity into money and the money back into commodity i.e. to the time it costs to transpose capital from one form into the other (Penguin *Grundrisse* 624–5).
The costs of circulation as such do not posit value, they are costs of the realization of values (Penguin *Grundrisse* 625).
All costs of circulation which arise only from changes in the forms of commodities do not add to their value. They are merely expenses incurred in the realization of the value or in its conversion from one form into another. The capital sent to meet those costs (including the labour done under its control) belongs among the *faux frais* of capitalist production. They must be replaced from the surplus-product and constitute, as far as the entire capitalist class is concerned, a deduction from the surplus-value or surplus-product, just as the time a labourer needs for the purchase of his means of subsistence is lost time (*Capital* 2.152; Penguin *Capital* 2.225–6).
Packing, sorting etc. Deduction from surplus-value (*Capital* 2.152; Penguin *Capital* 2.225–6).
See also Unproductive costs.

Cost of production

The cost of production consists of (1) raw materials and instruments of labour, that is, of industrial products the production of which has cost a certain amount of labour time, and (2) of direct labour, the measure of which is, precisely, time (*CW* 9.208 [*Wage Labour and Capital*, first published 1849]).

cost of production of labour

The amount of the means of subsistence required for the worker to maintain himself in a condition in which he is capable of working and to prevent the working class from dying out (*CW* 6.343 [*Principles of Communism*, written 1847]).
Cost of existence and reproduction of the worker (*CW* 9.209 [*Wage Labour and Capital*, first published 1849]).

Cost-price

Sum of the costs of production of the commodity (*Theories of Surplus Value* 2.220).
Component of the commodity-value (*Capital* 3.32; Penguin *Capital* 3.122).

cost-price of the commodity

Portion of the value of the commodity, which replaces the price of the consumed means of production and labour-power, only replaces what the commodity costs the capitalist himself (*Capital* 3.26; Penguin *Capital* 3.118).
What the commodity costs the capitalist and its actual production cost are two quite different magnitudes. That portion of the commodity-value making up the surplus-value does not cost the capitalist anything simply because it costs the labourer unpaid labour. Yet, on the basis of capitalist production, after the labourer enters the production process he himself constitutes an ingredient of operating productive capital, which belongs to the capitalist. Therefore, the capitalist is the actual producer of the commodity. For this reason the cost-price of the commodity necessarily appears to the capitalist as the actual cost of the commodity. If we take k to be the cost-price, the formula $C = c + v + s$ turns into the formula $C = k + s$, that is, the commodity-value = cost-price + surplus-value. . . . The category of cost-price, on the other hand, has nothing to do with the formation of commodity-

value, or with the process of self-expansion of capital (*Capital* 3.26–8; *Penguin Capital* 3.118–19).

The cost-price is equal to the value of the constant capital, the advanced means of production, plus the value of labour-power (*Capital* 3.870; Penguin *Capital* 3.1010).

See also Price of production.

Cottage industry

Sphere in which capital conducts its exploitation in the background of modern mechanical industry (*Capital* 1.438; Penguin *Capital* 1.595).

Credit

Credit is the *economic* judgment on the *morality* of a man. In credit, the *man* himself, instead of metal or paper, has become the *mediator* of exchange, not however as a man, but as the *mode of existence of capital* and interest . . . it is not the case that money is transcended in man, but that man himself is turned into *money*, or money is *incorporated* in him. *Human individuality*, human *morality* itself, has become both an object of commerce and the *material* in which money exists. Instead of money, or paper, it is my own personal existence, my flesh and blood, my social virtue and importance, which constitutes the material, corporeal form of the *spirit of money*. Credit no longer resolves the value of money into money but into human flesh and the human heart (*CW* 3.215 [*Notes on James Mill*, written 1844]).

Credit depends on the confidence that the exploitation of wage labour by capital, of the proletariat by the bourgeoisie, of the petty bourgeois by the big bourgeois, will continue in the traditional manner (*CW* 8.170 [*Bourgeoisie and Counter-Revolution*, first published 1848]).

A form in which capital tries to posit itself as distinct from the individual capitals, or the individual capital tries to posit itself as capital as distinct from its quantitative barrier (Penguin *Grundrisse* 659).

A new element of concentration of capital (Penguin *Grundrisse* 659).

45

Most powerful lever of centralization (*Capital* 1.587; Penguin *Capital* 1.779).

A new and terrible weapon in the battle of competition (*Capital* 1.587; Penguin *Capital* 1.778).

See also Over-production.

commercial credit

The credit which the capitalists engaged in reproduction give to one another (*Capital* 3.479; Penguin *Capital* 3.610).

Credit-capital

Capital of other people (*Capital* 3.512; Penguin *Capital* 3.645).

Credit system

An immanent form of the capitalist mode of production, and a driving force in its development (*Capital* 3.606; Penguin *Capital* 3.742).

One of the most effective vehicles of crises and swindle (*Capital* 3.607; Penguin *Capital* 3.742).

A powerful lever during the transition from the capitalist mode of production to the mode of production of associated labour (*Capital* 3.607; Penguin *Capital* 3.743).

Crime

Struggle of the isolated individual against the predominant relations (*CW* 5.330 [*German Ideology*, written 1845–6]).

Crises

There is, perhaps, no point in Political Economy in which there exists more popular misapprehension than on the power which banks of issue are commonly supposed to wield, of affecting general prices through an expansion or contraction of currency. The idea that the banks had unduly expanded the currency, thus producing an inflation of prices violently to be readjusted by a final collapse, is too cheap a method of accounting for every crisis not to be eagerly caught at. The question, be it understood, is not whether banks may be instrumental in fostering a fictitious system of credit; but whether they possess the power of determining the amount of circulation in the hands of the public. . . . The amount of notes in circulation is beyond the control of the banks themselves, and was actually contracting during the very epoch when trade expanded, and general prices underwent a process of inflation, resulting in a collapse. The vulgar notion, therefore, which refers the recent crisis, and crises generally, to an over-issue of bank notes, must be discarded as altogether imaginary (*CW* 16.8,12 [*Commercial Crises*, first published 1858]).

As a matter of principle in Political Economy, the figures of a single year must never be taken as the basis for formulating general laws. We must always take the average of from six to seven years, a period during which modern industry passes through the successive phases of prosperity, overproduction, crisis, thus completing the inevitable cycle (*CW* 6.458 [*Free Trade*, first published 1848]).

The stupendous productivity developing under the capitalist mode of production relative to population, and the increase, if not in the same proportion, of capital-values (not just of their material substance), which grow much more rapidly than the population, contradict the basis, which constantly narrows in relation to the expanding wealth, and for which all this immense productiveness works. They also contradict the conditions under which this swelling capital augments its value. Hence the crises (*Capital* 3.266; Penguin *Capital* 3.375).

A violent interruption of the labour-process (*Capital* 1.200; Penguin *Capital* 1.315).

Momentary and forcible solutions of the existing contradictions (*Capital* 3.249; Penguin *Capital* 3.357).

Violent eruptions which for a time restore the disturbed equilibrium (*Capital* 3.249; Penguin *Capital* 3.357).

commercial crises

Almost every trade crisis in our time has involved a violation of the correct proportion between fluid and fixed capital (*Werke* 12.33 [*Crédit mobilier*, first published 1856]).

monetary crises

A phase of every industrial and commercial crisis (*Capital* 1.137; Penguin *Capital* 1.236).

47

The monetary crisis consists primarily in the fact that all 'wealth' suddenly becomes depreciated in relation to the means of exchange and loses its 'power' over money. A crisis is in existence precisely when one can no longer pay with one's 'wealth', but must pay with money. And this again does not happen because of a shortage of money, as is imagined by the petty bourgeois who judges the crisis by his personal difficulties, but because the specific difference becomes fixed between money as the universal commodity, the 'marketable property and property in circulation', and all the other, particular commodities, which suddenly cease to be marketable property (*CW* 5.396–7 [*German Ideology*, written 1845–6]).

Cultivation (intensive)

The concentration of capital upon the same plot rather than its distribution among several adjoining pieces of land (*Capital* 3.675; Penguin *Capital* 3.813).

D

Death

Death seems to be a harsh victory of the species over the particular individual and to contradict their unity. But the particular individual is only a particular species-being, and as such mortal (*CW* 3.299 [*Economic and Philosophical Manuscripts*, written 1844]).
See also Life.

Degree of concentration (of labour)

Condensation of a greater mass of labour into a given period (*Capital* 1.386; Penguin *Capital* 1.534).

Degree of productivity

An important factor in the accumulation of capital (*Capital* 1.566; Penguin *Capital* 1.752).

Democracy

A transitional stage, though not towards a new, improved aristocracy, but towards real human freedom (*CW* 3.466 [*Condition of England*, first published 1844 E]).
The French Revolution was the rise of democracy in Europe. Democracy is, as I take all forms of government to be, a contradiction in itself, an untruth, nothing but hypocrisy (theology, as we Germans call it), at the bottom (*CW* 3.393 [*Social Reform*, first published 1843 E]).

Dependence (all-round)

All-round dependence, this primary natural form of the world-historical cooperation of individuals (*CW* 5.51 [*German Ideology*, written 1845–6]).

Development *See* Abundance; Accumulation; Communism; Dialectic; Freedom; Instrument of labour; Production; Productive power; Rate of profit, equalization of; Wealth.

progress

Progress may be measured by the relative increase of constant capital in relation to variable capital (*Capital* 3.759; Penguin *Capital* 3.894).

Dialectic

Science of the general laws of motion and development of nature, human society and thought (*Anti-Dühring* 169 E).

Science of universal interconnection (*Dialectics of Nature* 27 E).

Reflection of the motion through opposites which asserts itself everywhere in nature, and which by the continual conflict of the opposites and their final passage into one another, or into higher forms, determines the life of nature (*Dialectics of Nature* 280 E).

The reflection of the actual development going on in the world of nature and of human history in obedience to dialectical forms (*SC* 439 [to Schmidt, 1 November 1891 E]).

My dialectic method is not only different from the Hegelian, but is its direct opposite. To Hegel, the life-process of the human brain, i.e. the process of thinking, which, under the name of 'the Idea,' he even transforms into an independent subject, is the demiurgos of the real world, and the real world is only the external, phenomenal form of 'the Idea.' With me, on the contrary, the ideal is nothing else than the material world reflected by the human mind, and translated into forms of thought.

The mystifying side of Hegelian dialectic I criticised nearly thirty years ago, at a time when it was still the fashion. But just as I was working at the first volume of *Das Kapital*, it was the good pleasure of the peevish, arrogant, mediocre epigones who now talk large in cultured Germany, to treat Hegel in same way as the brave Moses Mendelssohn in Lessing's time treated Spinoza, i.e. as a 'dead dog.' I therefore openly avowed myself the pupil of that mighty thinker, and even here and there, in the chapter on the theory of value, coquetted with the modes of expression peculiar to him. The mystification which dialectic suffers in Hegel's hands, by no means prevents him from being the first to present its general form of working in a comprehensive and conscious manner. With him it is standing on its head. It must be turned right side up again, if you would discover the rational kernel within the mystical shell.

In its mystified form, dialectic became the fashion in Germany, because it seemed to transfigure and to glorify the existing state of things. In its rational form it is a scandal and abomination to bourgeoisdom and its doctrinaire professors, because it includes in its comprehension and affirmative recognition of the existing state of things, at the same time also, the recognition of the negation of that state, of its inevitable breaking up; because it regards every historically developed social form as in fluid movement, and therefore takes into account its transient nature not less than its momentary existence; because it lets nothing impose upon it, and is in its essence critical and revolutionary (*Capital* 1.29; Penguin *Capital* 1.102–3).

See also Law; Nature.

dialectic and formal logic

Even formal logic is primarily a method of arriving at new results, of advancing from the known to the unknown – and dialectics is the same, only much more eminently so; moreover, since it forces its way beyond the narrow horizon of formal logic, it contains the germ of a more comprehensive view of the world (*Anti-Dühring* 161 E).

Hegelian dialectic

The last word in philosophy (*Werke* 29.561 [to Lassalle, 31 May 1858]).

The basic form of all dialectics, but only after it has been stripped of its mystical form (*SC* 199 [to Kugelmann, 6 March 1868]).

Dictatorship (of the proletariat)   *See* Proletariat, dictatorship of.

See Communism; Proletariat; Republic (democratic); State.

Distribution

Itself a product of production, not only with respect to the object, [i.e.] that only the results of production can be distributed, but also with respect to the form, [i.e.] that the determinate way of sharing in production determines the particular forms of distribution, the form in which sharing takes place in distribution (*Texts on Method* 65–6 [*Introduction to the Grundrisse*, written 1857]).

Division of labour

The economic expression of the social character of labour within the estrangement. Or, since labour is only an expression of human activity within alienation, of the manifestation of life as the alienation of life, the division of labour, too, is therefore nothing else but the estranged, alienated positing of human activity as a real activity of the species or as activity of man as a species-being (*CW* 3.317 [*Economic and Philosophical Manuscripts*, written 1844]).
Estranged and alienated form of human activity as an activity of the species (*CW* 3.317 [*Economic and Philosophical Manuscripts*, written 1844]).
One of the chief forces of history up to now (*CW* 5.59 [*German Ideology*, written 1845–6]).
A necessary condition for the production of commodities (*Capital* 1.49; Penguin *Capital* 1.132).
The division of labour as the aggregate of all the different types of productive activity constitutes the totality of the physical aspects of social labour as labour producing use-values. But it exists as such – as regards commodities and the exchange process – only in its results, in the variety of the commodities themselves (*Contribution to Critique of Political Economy* 51).
Breaking down of the particular labour which produces a definite commodity into a series of simple and coordinated operations (*Theories of Surplus Value* 3.268).
Separation of occupations (*Theories of Surplus Value* 3.268).
Fundamental cause of the crippling of labour (*Werke* 39.441 [to Hirsch, 19 March 1895 E]).

See also Communism; Market; Pauperism; Relations, economic; Town.

division between mental and physical labour *See* Communism; Town.

division of labour in manufacture

Specific capitalist form of the social process of production (*Capital* 1.344; Penguin *Capital* 1.486).

A particular method of begetting relative surplus-value, or of augmenting at the expense of the labourer the self-expansion of capital (*Capital* 1.344; Penguin *Capital* 1.486).

Progress historically and a necessary phase in the economic development of society (*Capital* 1.344; Penguin *Capital* 1.486).

A refined and civilised method of exploitation (*Capital* 1.344; Penguin *Capital* 1.486).

social division of labour

The foundation of all production of commodities (*Capital* 1.331; Penguin *Capital* 1.471).

In a community, the produce of which in general takes the form of commodities, i.e. in a community of commodity producers, this qualitative difference between the useful forms of labour that are carried on independently by individual producers, each on their own account, develops into a complex system, a social division of labour (*Capital* 1.49–50; Penguin *Capital* 1.133).

See also Commodity-capital.

social division of labour and manufacturing

The less authority presides over the division of labour inside society, the more the division of labour develops inside the workshop, and the more it is subjected there to the authority of a single person. Thus authority in the workshop and authority in society, in relation to the division of labour, are in inverse ratio to each other (*CW* 6.185 [*Poverty of Philosophy*, first published 1847]).

The division of labour in the workshop implies concentration of the means of production in the hands of one capitalist, the division of labour in society implies their dispersion among

53

many independent producers of commodities. . . . Division of labour within the workshop implies the undisputed authority of the capitalist over men, that are but parts of a mechanism that belongs to him. The division of labour within the society brings into contact independent commodity-producers, who acknowledge no other authority but that of competition, of the coercion exerted by the pressure of their mutual interests; just as in the animal kingdom, the *bellum omnium contra omnes* more or less preserves the conditions of existence of every species (*Capital* 1.336; Penguin *Capital* 1.476–7).

E

Earth

Not yet capital (*CW* 3.292 [*Economic and Philosophical Manuscripts*, written 1844]).

General, natural element (*CW* 3.292 [*Economic and Philosophical Manuscripts*, written 1844]).

Original instrument of labour. Repository of raw materials (Penguin *Grundrisse* 485).

Economically speaking, includes water (*Capital* 1.174; Penguin *Capital* 1.284).

Universal subject of human labour (*Capital* 1.174; Penguin *Capital* 1.284).

Original toolhouse (*Capital* 1.175; Penguin *Capital* 1.285).

Original field of activity of labour (*Capital* 3.825; Penguin *Capital* 3.964).

Realm of forces of Nature (*Capital* 3.825; Penguin *Capital* 3.964).

See also Instrument of labour; Land.

Economic base *See* Economy; History; Relations; Society; State; Structure, (economic).

Economic plan *See* Nationalization.

Economics

Economics deals not with things but with relations between persons, and, in the last resort, between classes; these relations are, however, always attached to things and appear as things (*SW* 1.374 [review of *Contribution to Critique of Political Economy*, first published 1859 E]).

political economy

Political economy, this science of wealth, is therefore simultaneously the science of renunciation, of want, of saving – and it actually reaches the point where it spares man the need of either fresh air or physical exercise. This science of marvellous industry is simultaneously the science of asceticism, and its true ideal is the ascetic but extortionate miser and the ascetic but productive slave (*CW* 3.309 [*Economic and Philosophical Manuscripts*, written 1844].

Political economy, in the widest sense, is the science of the laws governing the production and exchange of the material means of subsistence in human society. . . . The conditions under which men produce and exchange vary from country to country, and within each country again from generation to generation. Political economy, therefore, cannot be the same for all countries and for all historical epochs (*Anti-Dühring* 177 E).

Political economy as the science of the conditions and forms under which the various human societies have produced and exchanged and on this basis have distributed their products – political economy in this wider sense has still to be brought into being (*Anti-Dühring* 181 E).

The scientific insight into the economics of the period of capitalist production (*Anti-Dühring* 271 E).

That economy, which, since the time of W. Petty, has investigated the real relations of production in bourgeois society, in contradistinction to vulgar economy, which deals with appearances only, ruminates without ceasing on the materials long since provided by scientific economy, and there seeks plausible explanations of the most obtrusive phenomena, for bourgeois daily use, but for the rest, confines itself to systematising in a pedantic way, and proclaiming for everlasting truths, the trite ideas held by the self-complacent bourgeoisie with regard to their own world, to them the best of all possible worlds (*Capital* 1.85; Penguin *Capital* 1.174–5).

vulgar economy   See Mercantilism.

Economists

The scientific representatives of the bourgeois class (*CW* 6.177 [*Poverty of Philosophy*, first published 1847]).

political economists
Ideological representative of the capitalist (*Capital* 1.537; Penguin *Capital* 1.718).
Bourgeois theorists (*Capital* 3.170; Penguin *Capital* 3.270).

Economy

An economy . . . the material basis of the world (*Capital* 1.86; Penguin *Capital* 1.175).

Elections

Actual relation of actual civil society to the civil society of the legislature, to the representative element (*CW* 3.121 [*Critique of Hegel's Philosophy of Law*, written 1843]).
The immediate, direct relation of civil society to the political state (*CW* 3.121 [*Critique of Hegel's Philosophy of Law*, written 1843]).
The chief political interest of actual civil society (*CW* 3.121 [*Critique of Hegel's Philosophy of Law*, written 1843]).
See also Franchise.

Elements of production

Means of production and labour-power (*Capital* 2.361; Penguin *Capital* 2.433).

Emancipation

Reduction of the human world and relationships to man himself (*CW* 3.168 [*On the Jewish Question*, first published 1844]).
See also Communism; Revolution.

emancipation of the working class
The emancipation of the working classes must be conquered by the working classes themselves (*First International* 82 [*Provisional Rules*, written 1864]).

57

human emancipation

Only when the real, individual man re-absorbs in himself the abstract citizen, and as an individual human being has become a species-being in his everyday life, in his particular work, and in his particular situation, only when man has recognized and organized his '*forces propres*' as social forces, and consequently no longer separates social power from himself in the shape of political power, only then will human emancipation have been accomplished (*CW* 3.168 [*On the Jewish Question*, first published 1844]).

political emancipation

A big step forward. True, it is not the final form of human emancipation in general, but it is the final form of human emancipation within the hitherto existing world order (*CW* 3.155 [*On the Jewish Question*, first published 1844]).

Reduction of man, on the one hand, to a member of civil society, to an egoistic, independent individual, and, on the other hand, to a citizen, a juridical person (*CW* 3.168 [*On the Jewish Question*, first published 1844]).

England   *See* Great Britain.

Equality

Equality is man's consciousness of himself in the element of practice, i.e. man's consciousness of other men as his equals and man's attitude to other men as his equals (*CW* 4.39 [*Holy Family*, first published 1845]).

Unity of human essence, man's consciousness of his species and his attitude towards his species, the practical identity of man with man, i.e. the social or human relation of man to man (*CW* 4.39 [*Holy Family*, first published 1845]).

Essence

human essence

The essence of man is no abstraction inherent in each single individual. In its reality it is the ensemble of the social relations (*CW* 5.4 [*Theses on Feuerbach*, written 1845]).

58

See also Being; Consciousness; Man; Property; Species-being; Supersession.

Estate capital   *See under* Capital.

Exchange

A mediating moment between production and the distribution (with consumption) which is determined by production (*Texts on Method* 70 [*Introduction to the Grundrisse*, written 1857]). *See also* Barter.

Exchange-process

The real relation that exists between commodities (*Contribution to Critique of Political Economy* 41).

Exchange-value(s)

A quantitative relation, the proportion in which use-values are exchanged for one another (*Contribution to Critique of Political Economy* 28).
A mutual relation between various kinds of labour of individuals regarded as equal and universal labour (*Contribution to Critique of Political Economy* 35).
Material expression of a specific social form of labour (*Contribution to Critique of Political Economy* 35).
The surplus over necessary use-values that is destined for exchange (*Grundrisse* 899).
Abstract wealth (Penguin *Capital* 1.1033).
A quantitative relation, the proportion in which values in use of one sort are exchanged for those of another sort, a relation constantly changing with time and place. Hence exchange-value appears to be something accidental and purely relative (*Capital* 1.44; Penguin *Capital* 1.126).
Value-form common to all commodities (*Capital* 1.54; Penguin *Capital* 1.139).
See also Accumulation; Circulation; Commodity; Labour; Labour-power; Money; Use-value; Wealth.

Exchequer

In the language of political economy the police is called exchequer (*CW* 8.174 [*Bourgeoisie and Counter-Revolution*, first published 1848]).
See also Tariffs.

Expenses   *See* Unproductive costs.

F

Factory legislation

First conscious and methodical reaction of society against the spontaneously developed form of the process of production (*Capital* 1.451; Penguin *Capital* 1.610).
Necessary product of modern industry (*Capital* 1.451; Penguin *Capital* 1.610).

Family

The use of narcotics to keep the children still is fostered by this infamous [factory] system. . . . The children who grow up under such conditions are utterly ruined for later family life, can never feel at home in the family which they themselves found, because they have always been accustomed to isolation, and they contribute therefore to the already general undermining of the family in the working-class. A similar dissolution of the family is brought about by the employment of the children. When they get on far enough to earn more than they cost their parents from week to week, they begin to pay the parents a fixed sum for board and lodging. . . . In a word, the children emancipate themselves, and regard the paternal dwelling as a lodging-house, which they often exchange for another, as suits them.
In many cases the family is not wholly dissolved by the employment of the wife, but turned upside down. The wife supports the family, the husbands sits at home, tends the children, sweeps the room and cooks. . . . It is easy to imagine the wrath aroused among the working-men by this reversal of all relations within the family, while the other social conditions remain unchanged. . . . If the family of our present society is being thus dissolved, this dissolution merely shows that, at bottom, the binding tie of this family was not family affection, but private interest lurking under the cloak of a

61

pretended community of possessions (*CW* 4.437–9 [*Condition of the Working Class*, first published 1845 E]).

The third circumstance which, from the very outset, enters into historical development, is that men, who daily re-create their own life, begin to make other men, to propagate their kind: the relation between man and woman, parents and children, the family. The family . . . must then be treated and analysed according to the existing empirical data, not according to 'the concept of the family' (*CW* 5.42–3 [*German Ideology*, written 1845–6]).

The division of labour . . . in the family and the separation of society into individual families opposed to one another, simultaneously implies the distribution, and indeed the unequal distribution, both quantitative and qualitative, of labour and its products, hence property, the nucleus, the first form of which lies in the family, where wife and children are the slaves of the husband (*CW* 5.46 [*German Ideology*, written 1845–6]).

The difference between the individual as a person and whatever is extraneous to him is not a conceptual difference but a historical fact. This distinction has a different significance at different times – e.g. the estate as something extraneous to the individual in the eighteenth century, and so too, more or less, the family. It is not a distinction that we have to make for each age, but one which each age itself makes from among the different elements which it finds in existence, and indeed not according to any idea, but compelled by material collisions in life (*CW* 5.81 [*German Ideology*, written 1845–6]).

The dissolute bourgeois evades marriage and secretly commits adultery; the merchant evades the institution of property by depriving others of property by speculation, bankruptcy, etc. . . . But marriage, property, the family remain untouched in theory, because they are the practical basis on which the bourgeoisie has erected its domination, and because in their bourgeois form they are the conditions which make the bourgeois a bourgeois. . . . One cannot speak at all of the family 'as such'. Historically, the bourgeois gives the family the character of the bourgeois family, in which boredom and money are the binding link, and which also includes the bourgeois dissolution of the family. . . . The family continues to exist even in the nineteenth century, only the process of its dissolution has become more general, not on account of the concept, but because of the higher development of industry and competition (*CW* 5.180-1 [*German Ideology*, written 1845–6]).

However terrible and disgusting the dissolution, under the capitalist system, of the old family ties may appear, nevertheless, modern industry, by assigning as it does an important part in the process of production, outside the domestic sphere, to women, to young persons, and to children of both sexes, creates a new economic foundation for a higher form of the family and of the relations between the sexes. It is, of course, just as absurd to hold the Teutonic-Christian form of the family to be absolute and final as it would be to apply that character to the ancient Roman, the ancient Greek, or the Eastern forms which, moreover, taken together form a series in historical development. Moreover, it is obvious that the fact of the collective working group being composed of individuals of both sexes and all ages, must necessarily, under suitable conditions, become a source of humane development; although in its spontaneously developed, brutal, capitalistic form, where the labourer exists for the process of production, and not the process of production for the labourer, that fact is a pestiferous source of corruption and slavery (*Capital* 1.460; Penguin *Capital* 1.620–1).

The democratic republic does not abolish the antagonism between the two classes; on the contrary, it provides the field on which it is fought out. And, similarly, the peculiar character of man's domination over woman in the modern family, and the necessity, as well as the manner, of establishing real social equality between the two, will be brought out into full relief only when both are completely equal before the law. It will then become evident that the first premise for the emancipation of women is the reintroduction of the entire female sex into public industry; and that this again demands that the quality possessed by the individual family of being the economic unit of society be abolished (*SW* 501 [*Family, Private Property, State*, first published 1884 E]).

See also Community of women.

Farmer *See also* Bonapartism; Class; Tenant farmers; Weaving.

Faux-frais (of production)

[E.g.] taxes, the price for government services (Penguin *Capital* 1.1043).

Superficial, external and incidental nature [of these things] as far as they touch the capitalist process of production (Penguin *Capital* 1.1043).

See also Cost of circulation; Unproductive costs.

Fetishism

Fantastic form of a relation between things (*Capital* 1.77; Penguin *Capital* 1.165).

See also Economy.

Force

Force is the midwife of every old society pregnant with a new one (*Capital* 1.703; Penguin *Capital* 1.916).

The instrument with the aid of which social movement forces its way through and shatters the dead, fossilized political forms (*Anti-Dühring* 220 E).

Foreign trade

Basis of the capitalist mode of production (*Capital* 3.237; Penguin *Capital* 3.344).

See also Crises; Gold; Rate of profit; Relations (international).

An important fact in the process of accumulation, because it tends to increase the variety of use-values and the volume of commodities (*Theories of Surplus Value* 3.446).

Form

Necessary architectonics of conceptual formulations (*CW* 1.15 [letter to his father, 10–11 November 1837]).

See also, Capital, industrial; Use-value.

Franchise

The struggle for the franchise is merely an illusory form . . . in which the real struggles of the different classes are fought out

among one another (*CW* 5.46–7 [*German Ideology*, written 1845–6]).
See also Elections.

Fraternity

Fraternité, the brotherhood of antagonistic classes, one of which exploits the other, this *fraternité* which in February was proclaimed and inscribed in large letters on the façades of Paris, on every prison and every barracks – this *fraternité* found its true, unadulterated and prosaic expression in civil war, civil war in its most terrible aspect, the war of labour against capital. This brotherhood blazed in front of all the windows of Paris on the evening of June 25 [1848], when the Paris of the bourgeoisie held illuminations while the Paris of the proletariat was burning, bleeding, groaning in the throes of death. This brotherhood lasted only as long as there was a fraternity of interests between the bourgeoisie and the proletariat (*CW* 7.144–7 [*June Revolution*, first published 1848]).

Freedom

In fact, the realm of freedom actually begins only where labour which is determined by necessity and mundane considerations ceases; thus in the very nature of things it lies beyond the sphere of actual material production. Just as the savage must wrestle with Nature to satisfy his wants, to maintain and reproduce life, so must civilized man, and he must do so in all social formations and under all possible modes of production. With his development this realm of physical necessity expands as a result of his wants; but, at the same time, the forces of production which satisfy these wants also increase. Freedom in this field can only consist in socialized man, the associated producers, rationally regulating their interchange with Nature, bringing it under their common control, instead of being ruled by it as by the blind forces of Nature; and achieving this with the least expenditure of energy and under conditions most favourable to, and worthy of, their human nature. But it nonetheless still remains a realm of necessity. Beyond it begins that development of human energy which is an end in itself, the true realm of freedom, which, however, can blossom forth only with this realm of necessity as its basis. The shortening of the working-day is its basic prerequisite (*Capital* 3.820; Penguin *Capital* 3.958–9).

Control over ourselves and over external nature, a control founded on knowledge of natural necessity (*Anti-Dühring* 137 E).

Necessarily a product of historical development (*Anti-Dühring* 137 E).

See also Communism; Democracy; Freedom of the press.

Freedom of the press

The free press is the ubiquitous vigilant eye of a people's soul, the embodiment of a people's faith in itself, the eloquent link that connects the individual with the state and the world, the embodied culture that transforms material struggles into intellectual struggles and idealizes their crude material form. It is a people's frank confession to itself. . . . It is the spiritual mirror in which a people can see itself, and self-examination is the first condition of wisdom (*CW* 1.164–5 [*Freedom of the Press*, first published 1842]).

Free trade

Normal condition of modern capitalist production (*Werke* 21.362 [*Protection and Free Trade*, first published 1888 E]).

free trade and protectionism

Moreover, the Protective system is nothing but a means of establishing manufacture upon a large scale in any given country, that is to say, of making it dependent upon the market of the world; and from the moment that dependence upon the market of the world is established, there is more or less dependence upon Free Trade too. Besides this, the Protective system helps to develop free competition within a nation. Hence we see that in countries where the bourgeoisie is beginning to make itself felt as a class, in Germany for example, it makes great efforts to obtain Protective duties. They serve the bourgeoisie as weapons against feudalism and absolute monarchy, as a means for the concentration of its own powers for the realization of Free Trade within the country.

66

But, generally speaking, the Protective system in these days is conservative, while the Free Trade system works destructively. It breaks up old nationalities and carries antagonism of proletariat and bourgeoisie to the uttermost point. In a word, the Free Trade system hastens the Social Revolution. In this revolutionary sense alone, gentlemen, I am in favor of Free Trade (*CW* 6.465 [*Free Trade*, first published 1848]).

We are for Free Trade, because by Free Trade all economical laws, with their most astounding contradictions, will act upon a larger scale, upon a greater extent of territory, upon the territory of the whole earth; and because from the uniting of all these contradictions into a single group, where they stand face to face, will result the struggle which will itself eventuate in the emancipation of the proletarians (*CW* 6.290 [*Free Trade Congress*, first published 1847]).

Only under Free Trade can the mighty productive forces of steam, electricity and machinery be completely developed; and the quicker this development the earlier and more completely does the unavoidable consequence appear: the division of society into two classes, capitalists and workers; hereditary wealth on the one side, hereditary poverty on the other; excess of supply over demand . . . suffering of the greater part of the population on account of overproduction, which produces either periodic crises or chronic stagnation in trade . . . in short, society runs into a blind alley from which no exit is possible except through a thoroughgoing revolution in the economic structure which underlies society itself. From this standpoint Marx has made clear over forty years that capitalist society will lead very quickly to this blind alley whether through Free Trade or any other route (*Werke* 21.362,374 [*Protection and Free Trade*, first published 1888 E]).

G

Geography *See* Relations, economic.

Geology

Series of negated negations, a series of successive shatterings of old and deposits of new rock formations (*Anti-Dühring* 163 E).

Gold

The specific commodity which serves as standard of value and medium of circulation (*Contribution to Critique of Political Economy* 123).

Material aspect of abstract wealth (*Contribution to Critique of Political Economy* 124).

Material symbol of physical wealth (*Contribution to Critique of Political Economy* 124).

As measure of value, and as standard of price, money has two entirely distinct functions to perform. It is the measure of value inasmuch as it is the socially recognized incarnation of human labour; it is the standard of price inasmuch as it is a fixed weight of metal. As the measure of value it serves to convert the values of all the manifold commodities into prices, into imaginary quantities of gold; as the standard of price it measures those quantities of gold. . . . Only in so far as it is itself a product of labour, and, therefore, potentially variable in value, can gold serve as a measure of value (*Capital* 1.100–1; Penguin *Capital* 1.192).

Government

Power of one class to oppress another (*Werke* 27.318 [to Marx, 21 August 1851 E]).

Government securities

Not capital at all, but merely outstanding claims on the annual product of the nation (*Capital* 2.353; Penguin *Capital* 2.423).

Great Britain

Great Britain has seen developed on the grandest scale the despotism of capital and the slavery of labour (*CW* 13.61 [*Labor Parliament*, first published 1854]).

Gross income

The gross income is that portion of value and that portion of the gross product measured by it which remains after deducting that portion of value and that portion of the product of total production measured by it which replaces the constant capital advanced and consumed in production. The gross income, then, is equal to wages (or the portion of the product destined to again become the income of the labourer) + profit + rent (*Capital* 3.840; Penguin *Capital* 3.979).

Gross profit

Gross profit = interest plus profit of enterprise (*Capital* 3.373; Penguin *Capital* 3.496).
See also Interest; Profit of enterprise.

Ground rent   *See* Rent.

Growth (of productive capital)

Growth of the power of accumulated labour over living labour. Growth of the domination of the bourgeoisie over the working class (*CW* 9.215 [*Wage Labour and Capital*, first published 1849]).

H

Hand

Not only the organ of labour, it is also the product of labour (*Dialectics of Nature* 230 E).

Handicraft

Manufacture based on handwork (*CW* 6.79 [*Constitutional Question*, written 1847 E]).

Heart

Man's heart is a wonderful thing, especially when carried in the purse (*Capital* 1.218; Penguin *Capital* 1.336).

Hegel

Hegelian philosophy of history

The last consequence, reduced to its 'clearest expression', of all this German historiography for which it is not a question of real, nor even of political, interests, but of pure thoughts (*CW* 5.55 [*German Ideology*, written 1845–6]).
See also Dialectic.

History

History does nothing. . . . It is man, real, living man who . . . possesses and fights; 'history' is not, as it were, a person apart, using man as a means to achieve its own aims; history is nothing but the activity of man pursuing his aims (*CW* 4.93 [*Holy Family*, first published 1845]).
And as everything natural has to come into being, man too has his act of origin – history – which, however, is for him a known history, and hence as an act of origin it is a conscious

self-transcending act of origin. History is the true natural history of man (*CW* 3.337 [*Economic and Philosophical Manuscripts*, written 1844]).

History is nothing but the succession of the separate generations, each of which uses the materials, the capital funds, the productive forces handed down to it by all preceding generations (*CW* 5.50 [*German Ideology*, written 1845–6]).

The history of all hitherto existing society is the history of class struggles (*CW* 6.482 [*Communist Manifesto*, first published 1848]).

The process of evolution of man himself (*SW* 408 [*Socialism, Utopian and Scientific*, first published 1880 E]).

A series of class struggles (*SC* 303 [to Lavrov, 12–17 November 1875]).

See also Communism; Division of labour; Nature; Science.

materialist conception of history

The materialist conception of history starts from the proposition that the production of the means to support human life and, next to production, the exchange of things produced, is the basis of all social structure; that in every society that has appeared in history, the manner in which wealth is distributed and society divided into classes or orders is dependent upon what is produced, how it is produced, and how the products are exchanged. From this point of view the final causes of all social changes and political revolutions are to be sought, not in men's brains, but in changes in the modes of production and exchange. They are to be sought, not in the philosophy, but in the economics of each particular epoch (*Anti-Dühring* 316 E).

Political, legal, philosophical, religious, literary, artistic etc. development rests on the economic base. It is not that economic conditions are the sole active cause and everything else mere passive effect. Rather there is interaction on the basis of a prevailing economic necessity in the last instance. . . . Hence there is not . . . an automatic effect produced by economic conditions; rather men make their history themselves, but in a given milieu which conditions them; they do this on the basis of pre-existing relations, amongst which the economic are decisive in the last instance, though they may be influenced by other relations, political and ideological; yet in the last

instance they are decisive and constitute the sole guide to knowledge (*Werke* 39.206 [to Borgius, 25 January 1894 E]).
See also Materialism; Structure (economic).

social history

History of the individual development of men, whether they are conscious of it or not. Their material relations are the basis of all their relations. These material relations are only the necessary forms in which their material and individual activity is realized (*SC* 35 [to Annenkov, 28 December 1846]).

Hoard

The simplest form in which the additional latent money-capital may be represented (*Capital* 2.325; Penguin *Capital* 2.396).
Creation of money-capital existing temporarily in latent form and intended to function as productive capital (*Capital* 2.353; Penguin *Capital* 2.423).

Hoarding

Withdrawal of money from circulation and its concentration at certain points (*Grundrisse* 886).
Accumulation which results from the mere fact of the separation of purchase and sale, i.e. from the immediate mechanism of simple circulation itself; accumulation which results from the function of money as means of payment (*Grundrisse* 886).
Excess of existing wealth over immediate needs and future liability or involuntary reverses in trade (*Grundrisse* 886).
While hoarding, as a distinct mode of acquiring riches, vanishes with the progress of civil society, the formation of reserves of the means of payment grows with that progress (*Capital* 1.141; Penguin *Capital* 1.240).
Not additional new social wealth; it represents new potential money-capital, on account of the function for which it is hoarded (*Capital* 2.495; Penguin *Capital* 2.567).
Not an increment of production (*Capital* 2.496; Penguin *Capital* 2.568).
An element immanent in the capitalist process of production (*Capital* 2.497; Penguin *Capital* 2.569).

The accumulation of money as a hoard, i.e. here as that part of capital which must always be on hand in the form of money as a reserve fund of means of payment and purchase (*Capital* 3.319; Penguin *Capital* 3.435).

Finally, as concerns the formation of hoards which constitute reserve funds for means of purchase and payment, be it for home or foreign trade, and which also merely represent a form of temporarily idle capital, they are in both cases necessary precipitates of the circulation process (*Capital* 3.320–1; Penguin *Capital* 3.437).

Hypothesis

The form of development of natural science, in so far as it thinks, is the hypothesis (*Dialectics of Nature* 318 E).

I

Ideas

Abstract thinking that gives itself up and resolves on intuition (*CW* 3.344 [*Economic and Philosophical Manuscripts*, written 1844]).
Ideas can never lead beyond an old world order but only beyond the ideas of the old world order. Ideas cannot carry out anything at all. In order to carry out ideas men are needed who can exert practical force (*CW* 4.119 [*Holy Family*, first published 1845]).

Ideas (ruling)

Ideal expression of the dominant material relations, the dominant material relations grasped as ideas; hence of the relations which make the one class the ruling one, therefore, the ideas of its dominance (*CW* 5.59 [*German Ideology*, written 1845–6]).

Ideology

Occupation with thoughts as with independent entities, developing independently and subject only to their own laws (*SW* 618 [*Ludwig Feuerbach*, first published 1886 E]).
Process accomplished by the so called thinker consciously, it is true, but with a false consciousness. The real motive forces impelling him remain unknown to him; otherwise it simply would not be an ideological process. Hence he imagines false or seeming motive forces. Because it is a process of thought he derives its form as well as its content from pure thought, either his own or that of his predecessors. He works with mere thought material, which he accepts without examination as the product of thought, and does not investigate further for a more remote source independent of thought; indeed this is a

matter of course to him, because, as all action is mediated by thought, it appears to him to be ultimately based upon thought (*SC* 459 [to Mehring, 14 July 1893 E]).
See also Religion.

ideological forms in society

Politics, religion, art, philosophy etc. (*SW* 182 [Preface to *Contribution to Critique of Political Economy*, first published 1859]).
See also History; Revolution.

ideological outlooks

False conceptions of nature, of man's own being, of spirits, magic forces etc (*SC* 423 [to Schmidt, 27 October 1980 E]).

Imperialism

The most prostitute and the ultimate form of the state power which nascent middle-class society had commenced to elaborate as a means to its own emancipation from feudalism, and which full-grown bourgeois society had finally transformed into a means for the enslavement of labour by capital (*SW* 287 [*Civil War in France*, first published 1871]).

Independence   *See* Accumulation, of capital; Communism; Means of production.

Individual

The social being (*CW* 3.299 [*Economic and Philosophical Manuscripts*, written 1844]).
Particular species-being (*CW* 3.299 [*Economic and Philosophical Manuscripts*, written 1844]).
The positing of the individual as a worker, in this nakedness, is itself a product of history (Penguin *Grundrisse* 472).
See also Communism; Emancipation; Production; Society; Town.

Industry

The actual, historical relationship of nature, and therefore of natural science, to man (*CW* 3.303 [*Economic and Philosophical Manuscripts*, written 1844]).

Inheritance

Power which transfers the fruits of alienated labour through the property of the dead (*Werke* 16.367 [*Über das Erbrecht*, first published 1869]).
See also Property.

Instrument and material of labour

A machine that is undergoing repair, no longer plays the part of an instrument, but that of a subject of labour. Work is no longer done with it, but upon it (*Capital* 1.198; Penguin *Capital* 1.312).
From the point of view of the process of circulation, we have on one side the instruments of labour – fixed capital, on the other the material of labour and wages – circulating capital. But from the point of view of the process of labour and self-expansion, we have on one side means of production (instruments of labour and material of labour) – constant capital; on the other, labour-power – variable capital (*Capital* 2.220; Penguin *Capital* 2.294).

mechanical instruments of labour

The bone and muscles of production (*Capital* 1.176; Penguin *Capital* 1.286).

Instrument of labour

Objective means which subjective activity inserts between itself and an object, as its conductor (Penguin *Grundrisse* 298–9).
See also Raw material.
A thing, or a complex of things, which the labourer interposes between himself and the subject of his labour, and which

serves as the conductor of his activity (*Capital* 1.174; Penguin *Capital* 1.285).

In a wider sense we may include among the instruments of labour, in addition to those things that are used for directly transferring labour to its subject, and which therefore, in one way or another, serve as conductors of activity, all such objects as are necessary for carrying on the labour-process. These do not enter directly into the process, but without them it is either impossible for it to take place at all, or possible only to a partial extent. Once more we find the earth to be a universal instrument of this sort, for it furnishes a *locus standi* to the labourer and a field of employment for his activity. Among instruments that are the result of previous labour and also belong to this class, we find workshops, canals, roads, and so forth (*Capital* 1.176; Penguin *Capital* 1.286–7).

Material vehicles of fixed capital (*Capital* 2.162; Penguin *Capital* 2.239).

See also Capital, latent.

Instruments of production

natural and man-made instruments of production

Here, therefore, emerges the difference between natural instruments of production and those created by civilization. The field (water, etc.) can be regarded as a natural instrument of production. In the first case . . . individuals are subservient to nature; in the second, to a product of labour (*CW* 5.63 [*German Ideology*, written 1845–6]).

Insurance fund

The sole portion of revenue which is neither consumed as such nor serves necessarily as a fund for accumulation. Whether it actually serves as such, or covers merely a loss in reproduction, depends upon chance. This is also the only portion of surplus-value and surplus-product, and thus of surplus-labour, which would continue to exist, outside of the process of reproduction, even after the abolition of the capitalist mode of production (*Capital* 3.847; Penguin *Capital* 3.986).

See also Unproductive costs.

Intensification

intensification of labour
Immoderate lengthening of the working-day (*Capital* 1.385; Penguin *Capital* 1.533).
See also Labour, intensified; Productive power.

Interest

In regard to interest, two things are to be examined: Firstly, the division of profit into interest and profit. (As the unity of both of these the English cåll it gross profit.) The difference becomes perceptible, tangible as soon as a class of monied capitalists comes to confront a class of industrial capitalists. Secondly, capital itself becomes a commodity, or the commodity (money) is sold as capital. Thus it is said e.g. that capital, like any other commodity, varies in price according to demand and supply. These then determine the rate of interest (Penguin *Grundrisse* 851).
Mere fragment of surplus-value (*Capital* 1.551; Penguin *Capital* 1.734).
Just another name, or special term, for a part of the profit given up by capital in the process of functioning to the owner of the capital, instead of putting it into its own pocket (*Capital* 3.339; Penguin *Capital* 3.460).
If we want to call interest the price of money-capital, then it is an irrational form of price quite at variance with the conception of the price of commodities (*Capital* 3.353; Penguin *Capital* 3.475).
Portion which falls to the lender (*Capital* 3.353; Penguin *Capital* 3.475).
Fruit of capital as such, of the ownership of capital irrespective of the production process (*Capital* 3.374; Penguin *Capital* 3.497).
Qualitatively speaking, interest is surplus-value yielded by the mere ownership of capital; it is yielded by capital as such, even though its owner remains outside the reproduction process. Hence it is surplus-value realized by capital outside of its process. Quantitatively speaking, that portion of profit which forms interest does not seem to be related to industrial or commercial capital as such, but to money-capital, and the

rate of this portion of surplus-value, the rate of interest, reinforces this relation (*Capital* 3.377; Penguin *Capital* 3.500).

Interest is net profit, as Ramsay calls it, which the ownership of capital yields as such, either simply to the lender, who remains outside the reproduction process, or to the owner who employs his capital productively (*Capital* 3.379; Penguin *Capital* 3.502).

A relationship between capitalists, not between capitalist and labourer (*Capital* 3.382; Penguin *Capital* 3.506).

Expression of the fact that value in general – materialized labour in its general social form – value which assumes the form of means of production in the actual process of production, confronts living labour-power as an independent power, and is a means of appropriating unpaid labour; and that it is such a power because it confronts the labourer as the property of another (*Capital* 3.379; Penguin *Capital* 3.502-3).

The differences between credit price and cash price (*Capital* 3.518; Penguin *Capital* 3.650).

Simply a part of the profit established under a special name (*Theories of Surplus Value* 3.461).

Nothing but a part of the profit (which in its turn, is itself nothing but surplus-value, unpaid labour), which the industrial capitalist pays to the owner of the borrowed capital with which he 'works', either exclusively or partially. Interest is a part of profit – of surplus value – which, established as a special category, is separated from the total profit under its own name, a separation which is by no means based on its origin, but only on the manner in which it is paid out or appropriated (*Theories of Surplus Value* 3.470-1).

See also Profit, gross; Rate of interest.

commercial interest

Interest calculated by the money-lenders for discounts and loans within the commercial world (*Capital* 3.512; Penguin *Capital* 3.644).

interest and profit

The real difference between profit and interest exists as the difference between a moneyed class of capitalist and an industrial class of capitalists. But in order that two such classes may come to confront one another, their double existence presup-

poses a divergence within the surplus value posited by capital (Penguin *Grundrisse* 852).
See also Capitalist.

International

A great gain for the workers (*Werke* 33.381 [to Paul Lafargue, 19 January 1872 E]).
See Socialism.

Investment

Conversion of money into productive capital (*Capital* 3.111; Penguin *Capital* 3.207).

J

Judicial system

Indispensable guarantee of bourgeois property (*CW* 8.201 [*Prussian Counter-Revolution*, first published 1848]).
See also Property.

L

Labour

An expression of life (*CW* 5.482 [*German Ideology*, written 1845–6]).

A sacrifice of life (*CW* 9.202 [*Wage Labour and Capital*, first published 1849]).

A commodity which the labourer has made over to another (*CW* 9.202 [*Wage Labour and Capital*, first published 1849]).

The manifestation of a force of nature (*SW* 315 [*Critique of the Gotha Programme*, written 1875]).

A confirmation of life (*Capital* 3.815; Penguin *Capital* 3.954).

As useful activity directed to the appropriation of natural factors in one form or another, labour is a natural condition of human existence, a condition of material interchange between man and nature, quite independent of the form of society (*Contribution to Critique of Political Economy* 36).

Purposive, productive activity (*Capital* 3.825; Penguin *Capital* 3.964).

Positive, creative activity (Penguin *Grundrisse* 614).

The substance of value (*Capital* 1.46; Penguin *Capital* 1.129).

So far therefore as labour is a creator of use-value, is useful labour, it is a necessary condition, independent of all forms of society, for the existence of the human race; it is an eternal nature-imposed necessity, without which there can be no material exchanges between man and Nature, and therefore no life (*Capital* 1.50; Penguin *Capital* 1.133).

Man can work only as Nature does, that is by changing the form of matter. Nay more, in this work of changing the form he is constantly helped by natural forces. We see, then, that labour is not the only source of material wealth, of use-values produced by labour. As William Petty puts it, labour is its father and the earth its mother (*Capital* 1.50; Penguin *Capital* 1.133–4).

An expenditure of human labour-power (*Capital* 1.53; Penguin *Capital* 1.137).

Labour-power in use is labour itself (*Capital* 1.173; Penguin *Capital* 1.283).

Labour is, in the first place, a process in which both man and Nature participate, and in which man of his own accord starts, regulates, and controls the material reactions between himself and Nature (*Capital* 1.173; Penguin *Capital* 1.283).

A process of consumption (*Capital* 1.179; Penguin *Capital* 1.290).

Labour is the substance, and the immanent measure of value (*Capital* 1.503; Penguin *Capital* 1.677).

The use-value of labour-power (*Theories of Surplus Value* 3.178).

The prime basic condition for all human existence, and this to such an extent that, in a sense, we have to say that labour created man himself (*SW* 354 [*Ape to Man*, written 1876 E]).

See also Capacity for labour; Capital, variable; Conditions of labour; Consumption, productive and individual; Division of labour; Instrument and material of labour; Instrument of labour; Intensification, of labour; Price of labour; Process of creating value; Wage-labour; Wages; Working-day; Working-period; Working-period and working-day; Workhouses.

abstract and concrete labour

On the one hand, then, it is by virtue of its general character, as being expenditure of human labour-power in the abstract, that spinning adds new value to the values of the cotton and the spindle; and on the other hand, it is by virtue of its special character, as being a concrete, useful process, that the same labour of spinning both transfers the values of the means of production to the product, and preserves them in the product. Hence at one and the same time there is produced a two-fold result (*Capital* 1.194; Penguin *Capital* 1.308–9).

abstract general labour

Different use-values are, moreover, products of the activity of different individuals and therefore the result of individually different kinds of labour. But as exchange-values they represent the same homogenous labour, i.e. labour in which the individual characteristics of the workers are obliterated.

83

Labour which creates exchange-value is thus abstract general labour (*Contribution to Critique of Political Economy* 29).

abstract labour

The source of exchange-value (*Contribution to Critique of Political Economy* 36).

accumulated labour   *See* Labour, living.

actual labour

Expenditure of the labourer's life-energy (Penguin *Capital* 1.982).
Realization of the labourer's productive faculties (Penguin *Capital* 1.982).
Personal function of the labourer (Penguin *Capital* 1.982).

additional labour

This reconversion of profit into capital shows rather upon closer analysis that, conversely, the additional labour – which is always represented in the form of revenue – does not serve for the maintenance, or reproduction respectively, of the old capital-value, but for the creation of new excess capital so far as it is not consumed as revenue (*Capital* 3.848; Penguin *Capital* 3.987).

aggregate labour of society

Articles of utility become commodities only because they are products of the labour of private individuals or groups of individuals who carry on their work independently of each other. The sum total of the labour of all these private individuals forms the aggregate labour of society (*Capital* 1.77; Penguin *Capital* 1.165).

alienated labour

Labour in which man alienates himself is a labour of self-sacrifice, of mortification (*CW* 3.274 [*Economic and Philosophical Manuscripts*, written 1844]).

associated labour   *See* Credit.

average labour   *See* Labour, human.

concrete labour

It would be wrong to say that labour which produces use-values is the only source of the wealth produced by it, that is of material wealth (*Contribution to Critique of Political Economy* 36).

Labour in the use-values of the commodity (Penguin *Capital* 1.992).

See also Labour, abstract and concrete.

cooperative labour *See* Labour, universal.

dead labour

Something stagnant (*Capital* 1.206; Penguin *Capital* 1.322).

See also Capital; Value.

disposable labour *See* Wealth.

human labour

The expenditure of simple labour-power, i.e. of the labour-power which, on an average, apart from any special development, exists in the organism of every ordinary individual (*Capital* 1.51; Penguin *Capital* 1.135).

industrial labour

Subjection to capital (*CW* 6.494 [*Communist Manifesto*, first published 1848]).

intensified labour

Exceptionally productive labour operates as intensified labour; it creates in equal periods of time greater values than average social labour of the same kind (*Capital* 1.302; Penguin *Capital* 1.435).

labour as power over individuals *See* Town.

labour in common

Directly associated labour (*Capital* 1.82; Penguin *Capital* 1.171).

living labour

A means to increase accumulated labour (*CW* 6.499).

Labour-power in action (*Capital* 1.200; Penguin *Capital* 1.315).

85

Something flowing (*Capital* 1.206; Penguin *Capital* 1.322).
The force that creates value (*Capital* 1.294; Penguin *Capital* 1.425).
The sole source of surplus-value (*Capital* 3.149; Penguin *Capital* 3.248).

machine labour

Labour, which as industry develops, devolves more and more on machines (*CW* 5.393 [*German Ideology*, written 1845–6]).

objectified labour

The reduction of all kinds of actual labour to their common character of being human labour generally, of being the expenditure of human labour-power (*Capital* 1.72; Penguin *Capital* 1.159–60).
Labour of an average social quality (*Capital* 1.305; Penguin *Capital* 1.440).
Expenditure of average labour-power (*Capital* 1.305; Penguin *Capital* 1.440).
See also Capital; Use-value; Value.

object of labour

Objectification of man's species-life (*CW* 3.277 [*Economic and Philosophical Manuscripts*, written 1844]).

past labour   *See* Capital; Value.

productive and unproductive labour

The distinction between productive and unproductive labour depends merely on whether labour is exchanged for money as money or for money as capital (Penguin *Capital* 1.1047).

productive labour

Value-creating labour (Penguin *Grundrisse* 272).
Labour which produces capital (Penguin *Grundrisse* 305).
Labour itself is productive only if absorbed into capital, where capital forms the basis of production, and where the capitalist is therefore in command of production. . . . Labour, such as it exists for itself in the worker in opposition to capital, that is, labour in the immediate being, separated from capital, is not productive (Penguin *Grundrisse* 308).

An abbreviation for the entire complex of activities of labour and labour-power within the capitalist process of production (Penguin *Capital* 1.1043).

That labourer alone is productive, who produces surplus-value for the capitalist, and thus works for the self-expansion of capital. If we may take an example from outside the sphere of production of material objects, a schoolmaster is a productive labourer, when, in addition to belabouring the heads of his scholars, he works like a horse to enrich the school proprietor. . . . Hence the notion of a productive labourer implies not merely a relation between work and useful effect, between labourer and product of labour, but also a specific, social relation of production, a relation that has sprung up historically and stamps the labourer as the direct means of creating surplus-value. To be a productive labourer is, therefore, not a piece of luck, but a misfortune (*Capital* 1.477; Penguin *Capital* 1.644).

Only that labour is productive which creates a surplus-value (*Theories of Surplus Value* 1.46).

The productivity of capital consists in the fact that it confronts labour as wage-labour, and the productivity of labour consists in the fact that it confronts the means of labour as capital (*Theories of Surplus Value* 1.394).

Productive labour is only a concise term for the whole relationship and the form and manner in which labour-power figures in the capitalist production process (*Theories of Surplus Value* 1.396).

So when we speak of productive labour, we speak of socially determined labour, labour which implies a quite specific relation between the buyer and the seller of the labour (*Theories of Surplus Value* 1.396).

real labour

Purposive productive activity (*Contribution to Critique of Political Economy* 52).

simple labour   *See* Labour, human, skilled, skilled and unskilled.

skilled and unskilled labour

The distinction between skilled and unskilled labour rests in part on pure illusion, or, to say the least, on distinctions that have long since ceased to be real, and that survive only by virtue of a traditional convention; in part on the helpless condition of some groups of the working-class, a condition that prevents them from exacting equally with the rest the value of their labour-power. Accidental circumstances here play so great a part, that these two forms of labour sometimes change places. Where, for instance, the physique of the working-class has deteriorated, and is, relatively speaking, exhausted, which is the case in all countries with a well developed capitalist production, the lower forms of labour, which demand great expenditure of muscle, are in general considered as skilled, compared with much more delicate forms of labour; the latter sink down to the level of unskilled labour. Take as an example the labour of a bricklayer, which in England occupies a much higher level than that of a damask-weaver. Again, although the labour of a fustian cutter demands great body exertion, and is at the same time unhealthy, yet it counts only as unskilled labour. And then, we must not forget, that the so-called skill labour does not occupy a large space in the field of national labour (*Capital* 1.192; Penguin *Capital* 1.305).

skilled labour

Labour which rises above the general level, being labour of greater intensity and greater specific gravity (*Contribution to Critique of Political Economy* 31).

Simple labour raised to a higher power (*Contribution to Critique of Political Economy* 31).

Expenditure of labour-power of a more costly kind, labour-power whose production has cost more time and labour, and which therefore has a higher value, than unskilled or simple labour-power (*Capital* 1.191–2; Penguin *Capital* 1.305).

Skilled labour counts only as simple labour intensified, or rather, as multiplied simple labour, a given quantity of skilled being considered equal to a greater quantity of simple labour. Experience shows that this reduction is constantly being made (*Capital* 1.51; Penguin *Capital* 1.135).

social labour

Labour which manifests itself in exchange-value appears to be the labour of an isolated individual. It becomes social labour

by assuming the form of its direct opposite, of abstract universal labour (*Contribution to Critique of Political Economy* 34).
See also Labour, intensified.

surplus labour

During the second period of the labour-process, that in which his labour is no longer necessary labour, the workman, it is true, labours, expends labour-power; but his labour, being no longer necessary labour, he creates no value for himself. He creates surplus-value which, for the capitalist, has all the charms of a creation out of nothing. This portion of the working-day, I name surplus labour-time, and to the labour expended during that time, I give the name of surplus-labour (*Capital* 1.209; Penguin *Capital* 1.325).

total labour

Necessary labour and unpaid surplus-labour (*Capital* 3.834; Penguin *Capital* 3.973).

universal and cooperative labour

Incidentally, a distinction should be made between universal labour and cooperative labour. Both kinds play their role in the process of production, both flow one into the other, but both are also differentiated. Universal labour is all scientific labour, all discovery and all invention. This labour depends partly on the cooperation of the living, and partly on the utilization of the labours of those who have gone before. Cooperative labour, on the other hand, is the direct cooperation of individuals (*Capital* 3.104; Penguin *Capital* 3.199).

unproductive labour   See Labour, productive.

useful labour

Only as a result of this universal alienation of commodities does the labour contained in them become useful labour (*Contribution to Critique of Political Economy* 42).
In order to create value, labour must be expended in a useful manner (*Capital* 1.188; Penguin *Capital* 1.300).
The labour, whose utility is thus represented by the value in use of its product, or which manifests itself by making its

89

product a use-value, we call useful labour (*Capital* 1.49; Penguin *Capital* 1.132).

It functions as the subjective element of the labour-process (*Capital* 2.431; Penguin *Capital* 2.503).

Labour fund

Separate part of social wealth (*Capital* 1.571; Penguin *Capital* 1.759).

Part of social wealth, elastic and constantly fluctuating (*Capital* 1.570; Penguin *Capital* 1.758).

Labourer(s)

The great majority of the nation (*CW* 4.500 [*Condition of the Working Class*, first published 1845 E]).

Labour-power on a mass scale cut off from capital or from even a limited satisfaction [of their needs] (*CW* 5.49 [*German Ideology*, written 1845–6]).

Mere labour capacities (Penguin *Grundrisse* 769).

Seller of labour-power (*Capital* 2.375; Penguin *Capital* 2.447).

commercial labourer(s) *See* Class.

factory labourer(s) *See* Proletariat.

workers' party *See* Party.

working class *See* Class.

Labour-market *See* Market.

Labour-power

A commodity which its possessor, the wage-worker, sells to capital (*CW* 9.202 [*Wage Labour and Capital*, first published 1849]).

The life-activity the worker sells to another person in order to secure the necessary means of subsistence. Thus his life-activity is for him only a means to enable him to exist. He works in order to live. He does not even reckon labour as part of his life, it is rather a sacrifice of his life. It is a commodity which he has made over to another (*CW* 9.202 [*Wage Labour and Capital*, first published 1849]).

A commodity which has the peculiar property that its use is a source of new value, the creation of new value (*Werke* 16.237 [review of *Capital*, first published 1868 E]).

Capacity for labour (*Capital* 1.164; Penguin *Capital* 1.270).

The aggregate of those mental and physical capabilities existing in a human being, which he exercises whenever he produces a use-value of any description (*Capital* 1.164; Penguin *Capital* 1.270).

Peculiar commodity (*Capital* 1.172; Penguin *Capital* 1.279).

Mode of existence which the value of the original capital assumed when from being money it was transformed into the various factors of the labour-process (*Capital* 1.202; Penguin *Capital* 1.317).

A circulating component part of productive capital (*Capital* 2.211; Penguin *Capital* 2.285).

Personal condition of production (*SW* 321 [*Critique of the Gotha Programme*, written 1875]).

See also Capacity for labour; Consumption, individual; Labour, abstract and concrete, objectified, productive; Labourer(s); Money; Proletariat; Wages.

Labour-process

The useful labour, the work, that produces use-values. Here we contemplate the labour as producing a particular article; we view it under its qualitative aspect alone, with regard to its end and aim (*Capital* 1.190; Penguin *Capital* 1.302).

The elementary factors of the labour-process are (1) the personal activity of man, i.e. work itself, (2) the subject of that work, and (3) its instruments (*Capital* 1.174; Penguin *Capital* 1.284).

Means of reproducing as capital (in capitalistic production) (*Capital* 1.531; Penguin *Capital* 1.711).

See also Process of creating value.

Labour-rent   *See* Rent.

Labour-time

Time during which capital is held fast in the sphere of production (*Capital* 2.242; Penguin *Capital* 2.316).
See also Production-time; Value.

congealed labour time

The labour-time materialized in the use-values of commodities (*Contribution to Critique of Political Economy* 30).

necessary labour-time

The labour-time contained in a commodity is the labour-time necessary for its production (*Contribution to Critique of Political Economy* 31).
The sum of all the particular labour functions which the division of labour separates off (Penguin *Grundrisse* 526).
That portion of the working-day, then, during which this reproduction takes place, I call 'necessary' labour-time, and the labour expended during that time I call 'necessary' labour. Necessary, as regards the labourer, because independent of the particular social form of his labour; necessary, as regards capital, and the world of capitalists, because on the continued existence of the labourer depends their existence also (*Capital* 1.208; Penguin *Capital* 1.325).

socially necessary labour-time

The labour-time socially necessary is that required to produce an article under the normal conditions of production, and with the average degree of skill and intensity prevalent at the time (*Capital* 1.47; Penguin *Capital* 1.129).

Labour vouchers   *See* Money-capital.

Land

Inorganic nature as such, *rudis indigestaque moles* ['a rude and motley mass'], in all its primeval wildness (*Capital* 3.815; Penguin *Capital* 3.954).
The product of an historical and natural process (*Theories of Surplus Value* 2.245).

Landed property   *See* Property.

Language

Element of thought itself (*CW* 3.304 [*Economic and Philosophical Manuscripts*, written 1844]).

Element of thought's living expression (*CW* 3.304 [*Economic and Philosophical Manuscripts*, written 1844]).

The 'mind' is from the outset afflicted with the curse of being 'burdened' with matter, which here makes its appearance in the form of agitated layers of air, sounds, in short, of language (*CW* 5.43–4 [*German Ideology*, written 1845–6]).

Practical, real consciousness that exists for other men as well, and only therefore does it also exist for me (*CW* 5.44 [*German Ideology*, written 1845–6]).

Language, like consciousness, only arises from the need, the necessity of intercourse with other men (*CW* 5.44 [*German Ideology*, written 1845–6]).

The problem of descending from the world of thoughts to the actual world is turned into the problem of descending from language to life (*CW* 5.446 [*German Ideology*, written 1845–6]).

Neither thoughts nor language in themselves form a realm of their own; they are only manifestations of actual life (*CW* 5.447 [*German Ideology*, written 1845–6]).

The product of a community, just as it is in another respect itself the presence of the community (Penguin *Grundrisse* 490).

See also Consciousness.

Law   *See* Crises; Dialectic; Economy; Freedom; Free trade, and protectionism; Rate of profit, equalization of.

absolute general law of capitalist accumulation

The greater the social wealth, the functioning capital, the extent and energy of its growth, and, therefore, also the absolute mass of the proletariat and the productiveness of its labour, the greater is the industrial reserve army. The same causes which develop the expansive power of capital, develop also the labour-power at its disposal. The relative mass of the industrial reserve army increases therefore with the potential energy of wealth. But the greater this reserve army in proportion to the active labour-army, the greater is the mass of a consolidated surplus-population, whose misery is in inverse ratio to its torment of labour. The more extensive, finally, the lazarus-layers of the working-class, and the industrial reserve army, the greater is official pauperism (*Capital* 1.603; Penguin *Capital* 1.798).

Like all other laws the absolute general law of capitalist accumulation is modified in its working by many circumstances, the analysis of which does not concern us here (*Capital* 1.603; Penguin *Capital* 1.798).

dialectical laws

Real laws of development of nature, and therefore are valid also for theoretical natural science (*Dialectics of Nature* 84 E).

law of capitalist accumulation

The correlation between accumulation of capital and rate of wages is nothing else than the correlation between the unpaid labour transformed into capital, and the additional paid labour necessary for the setting in motion of this additional capital. It is therefore in no way a relation between two magnitudes, independent one of the other: on the one hand, the magnitude of the capital; on the other, the number of the labouring population; it is rather, at bottom, only the relation between the unpaid and the paid labour of the same labouring population (*Capital* 1.581; Penguin *Capital* 1.771).

law of commodity exchange

The commodity that I have sold to you differs from the crowd of other commodities, in that its use creates value, and a value greater than its own. That is why you bought it. That which on your side appears as a spontaneous expansion of capital, is on mine extra expenditure of labour-power (*Capital* 1.224; Penguin *Capital* 1.342).

law of commodity production

The productivity of labour is inversely proportional to the value created by it. This is true of the transport industry as well as of any other. The smaller the amount of dead and living labour required for the transportation of commodities over a certain distance, the greater the productive power of labour, and *vice versa* (*Capital* 2.153; Penguin *Capital* 2.227).

law of competition

The fundamental law in competition, as distinct from that advanced about value and surplus value, is that it is determined not by the labour contained in it, or by the labour-time in which it is produced, but rather by the labour-time in which it can be produced, or, the labour-time necessary for reproduction. By this means, the individual capital is in reality only placed within the conditions of capital as such, although it seems as if the original law were overturned. Necessary labour-time as determined by the movement of capital itself; but only in this way is it posited. This is the fundamental law of competition (Penguin *Grundrisse* 657).

law of population in the capitalist mode of production

The labouring population therefore produces, along with the accumulation of capital produced by it, the means by which it itself is made relatively superfluous, is turned into a relative surplus-population; and it does this to an always increasing extent (*Capital* 1.591; Penguin *Capital* 1.783).

law of supply and demand

If supply and demand regulate the market-price, or rather the deviations of the market-price from the market-value, then, in turn, the market-value regulates the ratio of supply to demand, or the centre round which fluctuations of supply and demand cause market-prices to oscillate (*Capital* 3.181; Penguin *Capital* 3.282).

Absolutely nothing can be explained by the relation of supply to demand before ascertaining the basis on which this relation rests (*Capital* 3.181–2; Penguin *Capital* 3.282).

If supply and demand balance one another, they cease to explain anything, do not affect market-values, and therefore leave us so much more in the dark about the reasons why the market-value is expressed in just this sum of money and no other. It is evident that the real inner laws of capitalist production cannot be explained by the interaction of supply and demand (quite aside from a deeper analysis of these two social motive forces, which would be out of place here), because

95

these laws cannot be observed in their pure state, until supply and demand cease to act, i.e. are equated (*Capital* 3.189; Penguin *Capital* 3.290–1).
See also Money, price of; Need.

law of the dialectic

The law of the transformation of quantity into quality and *vice versa*; The law of the interpenetration of opposites; The law of the negation of the negation (*Dialectics of Nature* 83 E).

law of the negation of the negation   See Negation of the negation.

law of the production of surplus value

Equal capitals which have set in motion equal quantities of labour equally divided into paid and unpaid labour produce the same mass of surplus value (*Capital* 2.304; Penguin *Capital* 2.375).

law of the tendency of the rate of profit to decline

The progressive tendency of the general rate of profit to fall is, therefore, just an expression peculiar to the capitalist mode of production of the progressive development of the social prod-uctivity of labour. This does not mean to say that the rate of profit may not fall temporarily for other reasons. But pro-ceeding from the nature of the capitalist mode of production, it is thereby proved a logical necessity that in its development the general average rate of surplus-value must express itself in a falling general rate of profit (*Capital* 3.213; Penguin *Capital* 3.319).

The drop in the rate of profit, therefore, expresses the falling relation of surplus-value to advanced total capital, and is for this reason independent of any division whatsoever of this surplus-value among the various categories (*Capital* 3.214; Penguin *Capital* 3.320).

The law of the progressive falling of the rate of profit, or the relative decline of appropriated surplus-labour compared to the mass of materialized labour set in motion by living labour, does not rule out in any way that the absolute mass of exploited labour set in motion by the social capital, and conse-quently the absolute mass of the surplus-labour it appropri-ates, may grow; nor that the capitals controlled by individual capitalists may dispose of a growing mass of labour and, hence, of surplus-labour, the latter even though the number of labourers they employ does not increase (*Capital* 3.216; Penguin *Capital* 3.322–3).

It is a relative decrease, not an absolute one, and has, in fact, nothing to do with the absolute magnitude of the labour and surplus-labour set in motion. The drop in the rate of profit is not due to an absolute, but only to a relative decrease of the variable part of the total capital, i.e. to its decrease in relation to the constant part (*Capital* 3.217; Penguin *Capital* 3.323).

Counter-acting influences. . . . There must be some counter-acting influences at work, which cross and annul the effect of the general law, and which give it merely the characteristic of a tendency, for which reason we have referred to the fall of the general rate of profit as a tendency to fall. The following are the most general counterbalancing forces:

– Increasing intensity of exploitation (by lengthening the working-day, intensifying labour, greater velocities of machinery) (*Capital* 3.232–3; Penguin *Capital* 3.339).

– Depression of wages below the value of labour-power; one of the most important factors checking the tendency of the rate of profit to fall (*Capital* 3.235; Penguin *Capital* 3.342).

– Cheapening of the elements of constant capital; bound up with the depreciation of existing capital (that is, of its material elements).

– Relative over-population.

– Foreign trade. Since foreign trade partly cheapens the elements of constant capital, and partly the necessities of life for which the variable capital is exchanged, it tends to raise the rate of profit by increasing the rate of surplus-value and lowering the value of constant capital (*Capital* 3.236; Penguin *Capital* 3.342–3).

law of the transformation of surplus value into profit

Surplus-value expressed as profit always appears as a smaller proportion than surplus-value in its immediate reality actually amounts to.

To the degree that capital has already appropriated living labour in the form of objectified labour, hence to the degree that labour is already capitalized and hence also acts increasingly in the form of fixed capital in the production process, or to the degree that the productive power of labour grows, the rate of profit declines (Penguin *Grundrisse* 762–3).

law of value

We see then that that which determines the magnitude of the value of any article is the amount of labour socially necessary, or the labour-time socially necessary for its production (*Capital* 1.47; Penguin *Capital* 1.129).

See also Price of production; Theory of value; Value.

law of value in its international application

But the law of value in its international application is yet more modified by this, that on the world-market the more productive national labour reckons also as the more intense, so long as the more productive nation is not compelled by competition to lower the selling price of its commodities to the level of their value (*Capital* 1.525; Penguin *Capital* 1.702).

Life

The expression of an intellectual activity which develops in all directions, in science, art and private matters (*CW* 1.11 [letter to his father, 10–11 November 1837]).

The mode of existence of protein bodies, the essential element of which consists in continual metabolic interchange with the natural environment outside them, and which ceases with the cessation of this metabolism, bringing about with it the decomposition of the protein (*Dialectics of Nature* 396 E).

Life, the mode of existence of an albuminous body, therefore consists primarily in the fact that every moment it is itself and at the same time something else; and this does not take place as the result of a process to which it is subjected from without, as is the way in which this can occur also in the case of inanimate bodies. On the contrary, life, the exchange of matter which takes place through nutrition and excretion, is a self-implementing process which is inherent in, native to, its bearer, albumen, without which the latter cannot exist (*Anti-Dühring* 101 E).

Life consists precisely and primarily in this – that a being is at each moment itself and yet something else (*Anti-Dühring* 145 E).

Life is therefore also a contradiction which is present in things and processes themselves, and which constantly originates and resolves itself; and as soon as the contradiction ceases, life, too, comes to an end, and death steps in (*Anti-Dühring* 145 E).

Our definition of life is naturally very inadequate, inasmuch as, far from including all the phenomena of life it has to be limited to those which are the most common and the simplest. . . . In order to gain an exhaustive knowledge of what life is, we should have to go through all the forms in which it appears, from the lowest to the highest (*Anti-Dühring* 101 E).

See also Consciousness; Emancipation, human; Means of life; Relations; Process of production; Unproductive costs.

organic life

Form of motion of matter (*Dialectics of Nature* 307 E).

productive life

Productive life is the life of the species. It is life-engendering life. . . . Life itself appears only as a means to life (*CW* 3.276 [*Economic and Philosophical Manuscripts*, written 1844]).

Loan-capital   *See* Accumulation, of loan capital; Capital; Revenue.

Logic

Mind's coin of the realm, the speculative or mental value of man and nature – its essence which has grown totally indifferent to all real determinateness, and hence unreal – alienated thinking, and therefore thinking which abstracts from nature and from real man: abstract thinking (*CW* 3.330 [*Economic and Philosophical Manuscripts*, written 1844]).

formal logic   *See* Dialectic.

Lumpenproletariat

Passively rotting mass thrown off by the lowest layers of old society (*CW* 6.494 [*Communist Manifesto*, first published 1848]). Scum of the depraved elements of all classes (*SW* 1.646 [Note to *Peasant War*, first published 1870 E]).

See also Pauperism.

Luxury goods

Absolutely necessary for a mode of production which creates wealth for the non-producer and which therefore must provide that wealth in forms which permit its acquisition only by those who enjoy (Penguin *Capital* 1.1046).

All production that does not serve the reproduction of labour-power (*Capital* 3.106; Penguin *Capital* 3.200–1).

M

Machine

Colossal assembly of instruments (*Theories of Surplus Value* 3.366).

Machinery

The most appropriate form of the use-value of fixed capital (Penguin *Grundrisse* 699).
The machine proper is therefore a mechanism that, after being set in motion, performs with its tools the same operations that were formerly done by the workman with similar tools (*Capital* 1.353; Penguin *Capital* 1.495).

Man

A species-being not only because in practice and in theory he adopts the species (his own as well as those of other things) as his object, but – and this is only another way of expressing it – also because he treats himself as the actual, living species; because he treats himself as a universal and therefore a free being (*CW* 3.275 [*Economic and Philosophical Manuscripts*, written 1844]).
The first object of man (*CW* 3.304 [*Economic and Philosophical Manuscripts*, written 1844]).
Human nature (*CW* 3.335 [*Economic and Philosophical Manuscripts*, written 1844]).
Not merely a natural being: he is a human natural being. That is to say, he is a being for himself. Therefore he is a species-being, and has to confirm and manifest himself as such both in his being and in his knowing (*CW* 3.337 [*Economic and Philosophical Manuscripts*, written 1844]).
Man is the immediate object of natural science; for immediate, sensuous nature for man is, immediately, human sen-

suousness (the expressions are identical) – presented immediately in the form of the other man sensuously present for him. Indeed, his own sense-perception first exists as human sensuousness for himself through the other man (*CW* 3.304 [*Economic and Philosophical Manuscripts*, written 1844]).

Man is directly a natural being. As a natural being and as a living natural being he is on the one hand endowed with natural powers, vital powers – he is an active natural being. These forces exist in him as tendencies and abilities – as instincts. On the other hand, as a natural, corporeal, sensuous, objective being he is a suffering, conditioned and limited creature. . . . Man as an objective, sensuous being is therefore a suffering being – and because he feels that he suffers, a passionate being (*CW* 3.336–7 [*Economic and Philosophical Manuscripts*, written 1853]).

Sovereign of nature (*CW* 12.132 [*British Rule in India*, first published 1853]).

Man is in the most literal sense a *zoon politikon*, not only a sociable animal, but an animal which can individuate itself only in society (*Texts on Method* 49 [*Introduction to the Grundrisse*, written 1857]).

Man appears originally as a species-being, clan being, herd animal – although in no way whatever as a *zoon politikon* in the political sense (Penguin *Grundrisse* 496).

Man himself, viewed as the impersonation of labour-power, is a natural object, a thing, although a living conscious thing (*Capital* 1.196; Penguin *Capital* 1.310).

A product of nature which has developed in and along with its environment (*Anti-Dühring* 49 E).

See also Accumulation; Being; Communism; Consciousness; Emancipation; Equality; Essence; Freedom; Labour; Materialism; Nature; Production; Revolution; Society; Supersession; Wealth.

Manual work   *See* Handicraft.

Manufacture

Branches of production which had outgrown the guild-system (*CW* 5.67 [*German Ideology*, written 1845–6]).

A productive mechanism whose parts are human beings (*Capital* 1.320; Penguin *Capital* 1.457).
The immediate technical foundation of modern industry (*Capital* 1.361; Penguin *Capital* 1.504).
See also Division of labour.

Market

labour market

A branch of the general market for commodities (*Capital* 1.166; Penguin *Capital* 1.273).

world market

In history up to the present it is certainly likewise an empirical fact that separate individuals have, with the broadening of their activity into world-historical activity, become more and more enslaved under a power alien to them (a pressure which they have conceived of as a dirty trick on the part of the so-called world spirit, etc.), a power which has become more and more enormous and, in the last instance, turns out to be the world market (*CW* 5.51 [*German Ideology*, written 1845–6]).
The basis and the vital element of capitalist production (*Capital* 3.110; Penguin *Capital* 3.205).

Marriage

A form of exclusive private property (*CW* 3.294 [*Economic and Philosophical Manuscripts*, written 1844]).
See also Property.

Materialism

The chief defect of all previous materialism (that of Feuerbach included) is that things, reality, sensuousness are conceived only in the form of the object, or of contemplation, but not as sensuous human activity, practice, not subjectively (*CW* 5.3 [*Theses on Feuerbach*, written 1845]).

103

contemplative materialism

Materialism which does not comprehend sensuousness as practical activity (*CW* 5.5 [*Theses on Feuerbach*, written 1845]).

Material space

An element of all production and all human activity (*Capital* 3.774; Penguin *Capital* 3.909).
Form of existence of matter (*Dialectics of Nature* 312 E).

Mathematics

Science of magnitudes (*Dialectics of Nature* 340 E).

Matter

Necessary quality of conceptual formulations (*CW* 1.15 [letter to his father, 10–11 November 1837]).
See also Life, organic; Material space; Motion; Spirit.

Means of consumption *See* Bourgeoisie; Labour-power; Money; Reproduction, simple.

luxuries

Articles which enter into the consumption of only the capitalist class (*Capital* 2.407; Penguin *Capital* 2.479).

necessities

Articles which enter into the consumption of the working-class (*Capital* 2.407; Penguin *Capital* 2.479).

Means of life

Objective prerequisites for the sustenance and effectiveness of labour-power (Penguin *Capital* 1.989).
The means of subsistence are a particular form of material existence in which capital confronts the worker before he acquires them through the sale of his labour-power (Penguin *Capital* 1.1004).
No part of the labour-process, which, apart from the presence

of effective labour-power, requires nothing but the materials and means of labour (Penguin *Capital* 1.1004).

The articles which are the precondition for the survival of the worker himself (Penguin *Capital* 1.1005).

That part of the social commodity-capital which passes into the consumption of the labourer (*Capital* 2.226; Penguin *Capital* 2.300).

Consumption goods (*Theories of Surplus Value* 2.472).

See also Labour-power.

Means of production

Objective conditions of labour (Penguin *Capital* 1.981).

Capital which consumes itself in the production process, or fixed capital, is the means of production in the strict sense. In a broader sense the entire production process and each of its moments, such as circulation – as regards its material side – is only a means of production for capital, for which value alone is the end in itself. Regarded as a physical substance, the raw material itself is a means of production for the product etc. (Penguin *Grundrisse* 690).

Formal determinations of use-value (Penguin *Capital* 1.979).

The object and the means of labour (Penguin *Capital* 1.979).

The objective conditions of production (Penguin *Capital* 1.980).

The material factors of the labour-process (Penguin *Capital* 1.1003).

Not just as the means for accomplishing work, but as the means for exploiting the labour of others (Penguin *Capital* 1.1019).

The material conditions of labour (Penguin *Capital* 1.1054).

Mode of existence which the value of the original capital assumed when from being money it was transformed into the various factors of the labour-process (*Capital* 1.202; Penguin *Capital* 1.317).

Products of previous labour (*Capital* 1.176; Penguin *Capital* 1.287).

The material in which labour-power, the value-creator, incorporates itself (*Capital* 1.207; Penguin *Capital* 1.323).

Buildings, machinery, raw material, store-houses, implements and utensils (*Capital* 1. 217,307; Penguin *Capital* 1.334–5, 441).

The material part of productive capital (*Capital* 2.33; Penguin *Capital* 2.116).

Nutriment for productive consumption (*Capital* 2.60; Penguin *Capital* 2.138).

The means of production become capital only in so far as they have become separated from the labourer and confront labour as an independent power (*Theories of Surplus Value* 1.408).

See also Accumulation, primitive; Capital; Means of life; Nationalization; Process of production; Reproduction, simple; Subjects of labour.

Mercantilism

Actual vulgar economy (*Capital* 3.784; Penguin *Capital* 3.920).

Merchant

Agent of circulation (*Capital* 3.272; Penguin *Capital* 3.384).
See Merchant capital.

Merchant capital

Capital functioning in the sphere of circulation (*Capital* 3.279; Penguin *Capital* 3.392).

Individualized form of a portion of industrial capital engaged in the process of circulation (*Capital* 3.298; Penguin *Capital* 3.412).

Premises for the concentration of money wealth (*Capital* 3.327; Penguin *Capital* 3.444).

Oldest form of capital (*Capital* 3.609; Penguin *Capital* 3.744).

The independent and predominant development of capital as merchant's capital is tantamount to the non-subjection of production to capital, and hence to capital developing on the basis of an alien social mode of production which is also independent of it. The independent development of merchant's capital, therefore, stands in inverse proportion to the general economic development of society (*Capital* 3.327–8; Penguin *Capital* 3.445).

In the case of merchant's capital we are dealing with a capital which shares in the profit without participating in its production (*Capital* 3.284; Penguin *Capital* 3.397–8).

Within capitalist production merchant's capital is reduced from its former independent existence to a special phase in the investment of capital, and the levelling of profits reduces its rate of profit to the general average. It functions only as an agent of productive capital. The special social conditions that take shape with the development of merchant's capital, are here no longer paramount. On the contrary, wherever merchant's capital still predominates we find backward conditions. . . . The complete rule of industrial capital was not acknowledged by English merchant's capital and moneyed interest until after the abolition of the corn tax etc. (*Capital* 3.327; Penguin *Capital* 3.444–5).

commercial capital

Mercantile capital, or money as it presents itself as merchant wealth, is the first form of capital, i.e. of value which comes exclusively from circulation (from exchange), maintains, reproduces and increases itself within it (Penguin *Grundrisse* 856).

Merchant capital (*Capital* 3.267; Penguin *Capital* 3.379).

Breaks up into two forms or sub-divisions, namely, commercial capital and money-dealing capital (*Capital* 3.267; Penguin *Capital* 3.379).

Merchant's capital (*Capital* 3.325; Penguin *Capital* 3.442).

That form of capital which developed directly out of circulation (*Capital* 3.328; Penguin *Capital* 3.446).

Originally merely the intervening movement between extremes which it does not control, and between premises which it does not create (*Capital* 3.330; Penguin *Capital* 3.447).

Merchant's capital is older than the capitalist mode of production, in fact, historically the oldest free state of existence of capital. . . . Since merchant's capital is penned in the sphere of circulation, and since its function consists exclusively of promoting the exchange of commodities, it requires no other conditions for its existence – aside from the undeveloped forms arising from direct barter – outside those necessary for the simple circulation of commodities and money (*Capital* 3.325; Penguin *Capital* 3.442).

The production process rests wholly upon circulation, and circulation is a mere transitional phase of production. . . . That form of capital – merchant's capital – which developed directly out of circulation appears here merely as one of the forms of capital occurring in its reproduction process (*Capital* 3.328; Penguin *Capital* 3.445–6).

Merchant's capital, when it holds a position of dominance, stands everywhere for a system of robbery, so that its development among the trading nations of old and modern times is always directly connected with plundering, piracy, kidnapping slaves, and colonial conquest; as in Carthage, Rome, and later among the Venetians, Portuguese, Dutch etc. . . . The trading nations of ancient times existed like the gods of Epicurus in the intermediate worlds of the universe or rather like the Jews in the pores of Polish society (*Capital* 3.330–1; Penguin *Capital* 3.447–9).

A transmuted form of a part of this capital of circulation constantly to be found in the market, ever in the process of its metamorphosis, and always encompassed by the sphere of circulation. We say a part, because a part of the selling and buying of commodities always takes place directly between industrial capitalists (*Capital* 3.268; Penguin *Capital* 3.380).

Commercial capital, therefore – stripped of all heterogeneous functions, such as storing, expressing, transporting, distributing, retailing, which may be connected with it, and confined to the true function of buying in order to sell – creates neither value nor surplus-value, but acts as a middleman in their realization and thereby simultaneously in the actual exchange of commodities, i.e. in their transfer from hand to hand, in the social metabolism (*Capital* 3.282; Penguin *Capital* 3.395).

Commercial capital is, therefore, nothing but the producer's commodity-capital which has to undergo the process of conversion into money – to perform its function of commodity-capital on the market – the only difference being that instead of representing an incidental function of the producer, it is now the exclusive operation of a special kind of capitalist, the merchant, and is set apart as the business of a special investment of capital (*Capital* 3.270; Penguin *Capital* 3.382).

Mind

human mind

The highest product of organic matter (*Dialectics of Nature* 32 E).

philosophical mind

The self-conscious, self-comprehending philosophic or absolute (i.e. superhuman) abstract mind (*CW* 3.330; [*Economic and Philosophical Manuscripts*, written 1844]).

Miser

While the miser is merely a capitalist gone mad, the capitalist is a rational miser (*Capital* 1.151; Penguin *Capital* 1.254).

Money

The God of practical need, self-interest (*CW* 3.169–70 [*On the Jewish Question*, first published 1844]).

The jealous God of Israel (*CW* 3.172 [*On the Jewish Question*, first published 1844]).

The universal self-established value of all things (*CW* 3.172 [*On the Jewish Question*, first published 1844]).

The procurer between man's need and the object (*CW* 3.323 [*Economic and Philosophical Manuscripts*, written 1844]).

The alienated ability of mankind (*CW* 3.325 [*Economic and Philosophical Manuscripts*, written 1844]).

The general confounding and confusing of all things – the world upside down – the confounding and confusing of all natural and human qualities (*CW* 3.326 [*Economic and Philosophical Manuscripts*, written 1844]).

Representation of the value of all things, people and social relations (*CW* 5.410 [*German Ideology*, written 1845–6]).

The means of all means (*CW* 8.26 [*Impeachment*, first published 1848]).

Medium of exchange, medium of circulation, means of purchase (*Contribution to Critique of Political Economy* 96, 98).

Suspended coin (*Contribution to Critique of Political Economy* 126).

Not just an object of the passion for enrichment, it is the object of it (*Contribution to Critique of Political Economy* 132).

Materialised social tie (*Grundrisse* 866).

'Impersonal' property (*Grundrisse* 874).

Purely abstract wealth (*Grundrisse* 894).

The general form of wealth (Penguin *Grundrisse* 273).

General objectification of labour-time (Penguin *Grundrisse* 168).

The realization of exchange-value (Penguin *Grundrisse* 246).

The first form in which exchange-value proceeds to the character of capital (Penguin *Grundrisse* 259).

Elementary precondition of capital (Penguin *Capital* 1.949).

A crystal formed of necessity in the course of the exchanges, whereby different products of labour are practically equated to one another and thus by practice converted into commodities (*Capital* 1.90; Penguin *Capital* 1.181).

The general alienation of commodities (*Capital* 1.111; Penguin *Capital* 1.204).

The form of manifestation of the value of commodities, or the material in which the magnitudes of their values are socially expressed (*Capital* 1.93; Penguin *Capital* 1.184).

The universal subject-matter of all contracts (*Capital* 1.139; Penguin *Capital* 1.238).

The universal medium of payment (*Capital* 1.142; Penguin *Capital* 1.242).

A constituent part of the aggregate social capital (*Capital* 2.358; Penguin *Capital* 2.430).

The form in which every individual capital appears upon the scene and opens its process as capital (*Capital* 2.358; Penguin *Capital* 2.430).

The purely fantastic form of commodities (*Capital* 3.516; Penguin *Capital* 3.648).

The point of departure for the formation of capital (Penguin *Capital* 1.975).

Portion of capital which the capitalist uses to purchase labour-power (Penguin *Capital* 1.982).

The transmuted form of these means of subsistence which the worker immediately transforms back into means of subsistence as soon as he receives it (Penguin *Capital* 1.983).

See also Capital; Crises; Velocity (of money); Wealth.

price of money

On what does the price of money depend? It depends on the relationship of supply and demand at a given time and upon the currently existing scarcity or abundance of money. On what does the scarcity or abundance of money depend? It depends on the state of industry at the particular time and on the stagnation or prosperity of commerce in general (*CW* 7.223 [*State Credit*, first published 1848]).

Money-accumulation fund

The existence of latent money-capital, hence the transformation of money into money-capital (*Capital* 2.87; Penguin *Capital* 2.165).

Money-capital

In the case of socialized production the money-capital is eliminated. Society distributes labour-power and means of production to the different branches of production. The producers may, for all it matters, receive paper vouchers entitling them to withdraw from the social supplies of consumer goods a quantity corresponding to their labour-time. These vouchers are not money. They do not circulate (*Capital* 2.362; Penguin *Capital* 2.434).

Capital-value in the state or form of money (*Capital* 2.28; Penguin *Capital* 2.112).

Form assumed by capital-value at the various stages of its circulation (*Capital* 2.50; Penguin *Capital* 2.133).

First depository of capital-value (*Capital* 2.28; Penguin *Capital* 2.112).

Form of existence of capital (*Capital* 2.31; Penguin *Capital* 2.115).

Retransformation of commodity-capital into productive capital (*Capital* 2.74; Penguin *Capital* 2.153).

Object of manipulation by a special kind of capitalist (*Capital* 2.425; Penguin *Capital* 2.497).

A transient form of capital – in contradistinction to the other forms of capital, namely, commodity-capital and productive capital (*Capital* 3.463; Penguin *Capital* 3.594).

See also Circuit, of money capital; Commodity-capital; Circulation-capital.

Money-crisis *See* Crisis.

Money-dealing capital

The purely technical movements performed by money in the circulation process of industrial, and, as we may now add, of commercial capital (since it takes over a part of the circulation movement of industrial capital as its own, peculiar movement), if individualized as a function of some particular capital performing just these, and only these, operations as it specific operations, convert this capital into money-dealing capital (*Capital* 3.315; Penguin *Capital* 3.431).

functions of money-dealing capital

Paying and receiving money, settling accounts, keeping current accounts, sorting money, etc. (*Capital* 3.317; Penguin *Capital* 3.433).

Money-rent   *See* Rent.

Money-reserve fund

The part of fixed capital which is transformed into money and is gradually accumulated (*Capital* 2.167; Penguin *Capital* 2.243).

functions of the money-reserve fund

Sinking-fund, in which the value of the fixed capital flows back to its starting-point in proportion to its wear and tear (*Capital* 2.185; Penguin *Capital* 2.261).
Work of maintenance and repair (costs of maintenance) (*Capital* 2.180–1; Penguin *Capital* 2.256–7).
Insurance etc. (*Capital* 2.180; Penguin *Capital* 2.256).

Monopoly

The opposite of competition is monopoly. Monopoly was the war-cry of the Mercantilists (*CW* 3.432 [*Outlines*, first published 1844 E]).

Motion

Motion in the most general sense, conceived as the mode of existence, the inherent attribute, of matter, comprehends all changes and processes occurring in the universe, from mere change of place right up to thinking (*Dialectics of Nature* 92 E). The mode of existence of matter (*Anti-Dühring* 75 E).

Movement in circuits

Capital's movement in circuits is therefore the unity of circulation and production (*Capital* 2.60; Penguin *Capital* 2.139).

circular movement of capital

The circular movement of capital takes place in three stages, which . . . form the following series:

First stage: The capitalist appears as a buyer on the commodity- and the labour-market; his money is transformed into commodities, or it goes through the circulation act M-C.

Second stage: Productive consumption of the purchased commodities by the capitalist. He acts as a capitalist producer of commodities; his capital passes through the process of production. The result is a commodity of more value than that of the elements entering into its production.

Third stage: The capitalist returns to the market as a seller; his commodities are turned into money, or they pass through the circulation act C-M (*Capital* 2.25; Penguin *Capital* 2.109).

N

Nation

The whole of society (*Capital* 3.438 E; Penguin *Capital* 3.569 E).

National workshops

In their appellation, though not in their content, the *national ateliers* were the embodied protest of the proletariat against bourgeois industry, bourgeois credit and the bourgeois republic. The whole hate of the bourgeoisie was, therefore, turned upon them (*CW* 10.63 [*Class Struggles in France*, first published 1850]).

Nationalization

The nationalization of land will work a complete change in the relations between labour and capital, and finally, do away with the capitalist form of production, whether industrial or rural. Then class distinctions and privileges will disappear together with the economical basis upon which they rest. To live on other people's labour will become a thing of the past. There will be no longer any government or state power, distinct from society itself! Agriculture, mining, manufacture, in one word, all branches of production will gradually be organized in the most adequate manner. National centralization of the means of production will become the national basis of a society composed of associations of free and equal producers, carrying on the social business on a common and rational plan. Such is the humanitarian goal to which the great economic movement of the nineteenth century is tending (*International Herald* (London) 15 June 1872).

Natural elements

Natural elements entering as agents into production, and which cost nothing, no matter what role they play in production, do not enter as components of capital, but as a free gift of Nature to capital, that is, as a free gift of Nature's productive power to labour, which, however, appears as the productiveness of capital, as all other productivity under the capitalist mode of production (*Capital* 3.745; Penguin *Capital* 3.879).
See also Conditions, material; Physical conditions.

Natural force

Not itself a product of labour.
Natural production agent.
E.g. the motive power of the waterfall (*Capital* 3.643; Penguin *Capital* 3.782).
Not the source of surplus-profit, but only its natural basis (*Capital* 3.647; Penguin *Capital* 3.786).

Natural powers

E.g. air, light, electricity, steam, water (*Theories of Surplus Value* 2.43).
See also Labour; Wealth.

Nature

The nature which develops in human history – the genesis of human society – is man's real nature; hence nature as it develops through industry, even though in an estranged form, is true anthropological nature (*CW* 3.303 [*Economic and Philosophical Manuscripts*, written 1844]).
Material on which the worker's labour is realized, in which it is active, from which and by means of which it produces (*CW* 3.273 [*Economic and Philosophical Manuscripts*, written 1844]).
Man's inorganic body (*CW* 3.277 [*Economic and Philosophical Manuscripts*, written 1844]).
Proof of dialectics (*Anti-Dühring* 33 E).

See also Communism; Consciousness; Consumption; Dialectic; Freedom; Labour; Production; Science; Society; Wealth.

Necessity *See* Contingency; Freedom; Negation of the negation; Revolution.

Need

It is only where production is under the actual, predetermining control of society that the latter establishes a relation between the volume of social labour-time applied in producing definite articles, and the volume of the social need to be satisfied by these articles (*Capital* 3.187; Penguin *Capital* 3.288–9).

Production comes to a standstill at a point fixed by the production and realization of profit, and not the satisfaction of requirements (*Capital* 3.258; Penguin *Capital* 3.367).

'Social demand', i.e. the factor which regulates the principle of demand, is essentially subject to the mutual relationship of the different classes and their respective economic position, notably therefore to, firstly, the ratio of total surplus-value to wages, and, secondly, to the relation of the various parts into which surplus-value is split up (profit, interest, ground-rent, taxes, etc.). And this thus again shows how absolutely nothing can be explained by the relation of supply to demand before ascertaining the basis on which this relation rests (*Capital* 3.181–2; Penguin *Capital* 3.282).

From each according to his ability, to each according to his needs! (*SW* 321 [*Critique of the Gotha Programme*, written 1875]).

See also Communism; Freedom; Labour; Money; Wealth.

Negation

negation of the negation

An extremely general – and for this reason extremely far-reaching and important – law of development of nature, history, and thought; a law which, as we have seen, holds

good in the animal and plant kingdoms, in geology, in mathematics, in history and in philosophy (*Anti-Dühring* 168 E).
See also Communism.

negation of the negation of private property

The capitalist mode of appropriation, the result of the capitalist mode of production, produces capitalist private property. This is the first negation of individual private property, as founded on the labour of the proprietor. But capitalist production begets, with the inexorability of a law of Nature, its own negation. It is the negation of negation. This does not re-establish private property for the producer, but gives him individual property (*Capital* 1.715; Penguin *Capital* 1.929).

Nett income

Form in which the Physiocrats originally conceived surplus-value (*Theories of Surplus Value* 2.547).
Net revenue is therefore in fact the excess of the product (or the excess of its value) over that part of it which replaces the capital outlay, comprising both constant and variable capital (*Theories of Surplus Value* 2.547).
Surplus-value, and thus the surplus-product, which remains after deducting wages (*Capital* 3.840; Penguin *Capital* 3.979).

Nett product

The form of surplus-produce in which surplus-value is embodied (Penguin *Capital* 1.1050).

Nourishment

A form of consumption (*Texts on Method* 59 [*Introduction to the Grundrisse*, written 1857]).

Number of turnovers (of total social capital)

Number of turnovers made by the entire social capital is equal to the sum of the capitals turned over in the various spheres of production divided by the sum of the capitals advanced in those spheres (*Capital* 2.274; Penguin *Capital* 2.346).

O

Object

Confirmation of one of my essential powers (*CW* 3.301 [*Economic and Philosophical Manuscripts*, written 1844]).

Objectification *See* Accumulation, of capital; Communism; Labour, objectified; Means of production; Money; Production; Wage-labour; Wealth; Supersession.

objectification of labour-time

Product of universal alienation and of the supersession of all individual labour (*Contribution to Critique of Political Economy* 47).

Overpopulation *See* Pauperism.

Over-production

General overproduction would take place, not because relatively too little had been produced of the commodities consumed by the workers or too little of those consumed by the capitalists, but because too much of both had been produced – not too much for consumption, but too much to retain the correct relation between consumption and realization; too much for realization (Penguin *Grundrisse* 442–3).

The form in which overproduction is hidden is always more or less extension of credit (*Werke* 29.227 [to Marx, 11 December 1857 E]).

See also Free trade.

P

Pan-slavism

The union of all the small Slav nations and nationalities of Austria, and secondarily of Turkey, for struggle against the Austrian Germans, the Magyars and, eventually against the Turks (*CW* 8.233 [*Magyar Struggle*, first published 1849 E]).
Political swindle under the aegis of a non-existent slavic nationality (*Werke* 35.371 [to Kautsky, 7 February 1882 E]).

Party   *See* Communism.

workers' party

That section of the working class which has become conscious of the common class interest (*First International* 135 [*Prussian Military Question*, first published 1865 E]).
See also Communist.

Passion

Dominion of the objective being in me (*CW* 3.304 [*Economic and Philosophical Manuscripts*, written 1844]).
Sensuous outburst of my life activity (*CW* 3.304 [*Economic and Philosophical Manuscripts*, written 1844]).
The essential power of man energetically bent on its object (*CW* 3.337 [*Economic and Philosophical Manuscripts*, written 1844]).

Pauper

The proletarian whose whole energy has been sapped (*CW* 5.202 [*German Ideology*, written 1845–6]).
See also Proletariat.

Pauperism

The position of the ruined proletariat (*CW* 5.202 [*German Ideology*, written 1845–6]).

The lowest sediment of the relative surplus-population finally dwells in the sphere of pauperism. Exclusive of vagabonds, criminals, prostitutes, in a word, the 'dangerous' classes, this layer of society consists of three categories. First, those able to work. . . . Second, orphans and pauper children. These are candidates for the industrial reserve army. . . . Third, the demoralized and ragged, and those unable to work, chiefly people who succumb to their incapacity for adaptation, due to the division of labour; people who have passed the normal age of the labourer; the victims of industry, whose number increases with the increase of dangerous machinery, of mines, chemical works, etc. the mutilated, the sickly, the widows, etc. (*Capital* 1.602–3; Penguin *Capital* 1.797).

The hospital of the active labour-army and the dead weight of the industrial reserve army (*Capital* 1.603; Penguin *Capital* 1.797).

official pauperism

That part of the working-class which has forfeited its condition of existence (the sale of labour-power), and vegetates upon public alms (*Capital* 1.611; Penguin *Capital* 1.807).
See also Workhouses.

Period of production

The entire time of production required to finish a certain product (*Capital* 2.165; Penguin *Capital* 2.241).

Periods of turnover

The periods in which the value-substitute of the variable capital employed for a definite time can function anew as capital, hence as a new capital (*Capital* 2.316; Penguin *Capital* 2.387).

Philistinism (German)

Not a normal historical phase but an extreme caricature, a piece of degeneration (*SC* 414 [to Ernst, 5 June 1890 E]).

Philosophy

Form and manner of existence of the estrangement of the essence of man (*CW* 3.328 [*Economic and Philosophical Manuscripts*, written 1844]).
Philosophy and the study of the actual world have the same relation to one another as onanism and sexual love (*CW* 5.236 [*German Ideology*, written 1845–6]).
The philosophers have only interpreted the world in various ways; the point is to change it (*CW* 5.5 [*Theses on Feuerbach*, written 1845]).
Philosophy cannot be made a reality without the abolition of the proletariat, the proletariat cannot be abolished without philosophy being made a reality (*CW* 3.187 [*Introduction to Critique of Hegel's Philosophy of Law*, first published 1844]).
See also Spirit.

Physical conditions

External physical conditions fall into two great economic classes, (1) natural wealth in means of subsistence, i.e. a fruitful soil, waters teeming with fish etc., and (2) natural wealth in the instruments of labour, such as waterfalls, navigable rivers, wood, metal, coal, etc. At the dawn of civilization, it is the first class that turns the scale; at a higher stage of development, it is the second (*Capital* 1.480; Penguin *Capital* 1.648).
See also Conditions, material; Natural elements.

Physiocrats

The physiocratic doctrine of Dr. Quesnay forms the tradition from the mercantile system to Adam Smith. Physiocracy represents directly the decomposition of feudal property in economic terms, but it therefore just as directly represents its economic metamorphosis and restoration, save that now its

language is no longer feudal but economic (*CW* 3.292 [*Economic and Philosophical Manuscripts*, written 1844]).
First systematic conception of capitalist production (*Capital* 2.364; Penguin *Capital* 2.436).

Physiology

The physics and especially the chemistry of the living body, but with that it ceases to be specially chemistry: on the one hand its domain becomes restricted but, on the other hand, inside this domain it becomes raised to a higher power (*Dialectics of Nature* 339 E).

Piece-wages

Converted form of wages by time (*Capital* 1.516; Penguin *Capital* 1.692).

Police   *See* Security.

Political economy   *See* Economics.

Population

The basis and subject of the whole social act of production (*Texts on Method* 72 [*Introduction to the Grundrisse*, written 1857]).
See also Law, of population; Market.

Poverty

The passive bond which causes the human being to experience the need of the greatest wealth – the other human being (*CW* 3.304 [*Economic and Philosophical Manuscripts*, written 1844]).
See also Pauperism.

Pre-history   *See* Relations of production.

President

The elected National Assembly [of the French Second Empire] stands in a metaphysical relation, but the elected President in a personal relation, to the nation. The National Assembly, indeed, exhibits in its individual representatives the manifold aspects of the national spirit, but in the President this national spirit finds its incarnation. As against the Assembly, he possesses a sort of divine right; he is President by the grace of the people (*CW* 11.117 [*Eighteenth Brumaire*, first published 1852]).

Price

The converted form in which the exchange-value of commodities appears within the circulation process (*Contribution to Critique of Political Economy* 66).
The money-name of the labour realized in a commodity (*Capital* 1.103; Penguin *Capital* 1.195–6).

natural price of wage-labour

The price of labour that is not regulated by competition, but which, on the contrary, regulates the latter (*Capital* 3.864; Penguin *Capital* 3.1004).
See also Cost-price; Price of production; Value; Wages.

Price of labour

relative price of labour

Price of labour as compared both with surplus-value and with the value of the product (*Capital* 1.525; Penguin *Capital* 1.702).

Price of production

The prices which obtain as the average of the various rates of profit in the different spheres of production added to the cost-prices of the different spheres of production (*Capital* 3.157; Penguin *Capital* 3.257).

Their prerequisite is the existence of a general rate of profit (*Capital* 3.157; Penguin *Capital* 3.257).

The price of production of a commodity is equal to its cost-price plus the profit, allotted to it in per cent, in accordance with the general rate of profit, or, in other words, to its cost-price plus the average profit (*Capital* 3.157; Penguin *Capital* 3.257).

The elements of cost (the value of consumed constant and variable capital) plus a profit determined by the general rate of profit and calculated on the total advanced capital, whether consumed or not (*Capital* 3.640; Penguin *Capital* 3.779).

It is really what Adam Smith calls natural price, Ricardo calls price of production, or cost of production, and the physiocrats call *prix nécessaire*, because in the long run it is a prerequisite of supply, of the reproduction of commodities in every individual sphere (*Capital* 3.198; Penguin *Capital* 3.300).

Regulating market-price (*Capital* 3.655; Penguin *Capital* 3.794).

The law of value dominates price movements with reductions or increases in required labour-time making prices of production fall or rise (*Capital* 3.179; Penguin *Capital* 3.280).

Because the value of the commodity is determined by labour-time, the average price of the commodities . . . can never be equal to their value although this determination of the average price is only derived from the value which is based on labour-time (*Theories of Surplus Value* 2.34).

The transformation of values into prices of production serves to obscure the basis for determining value itself (*Capital* 3.168; Penguin *Capital* 3.268).

The price thus equalized, which divides up the social surplus-value equally among the individual capitals in proportion to their sizes, is the price of production of commodities, the centre around which the oscillation of the market prices move (*SC* 206 [to Engels, 30 April 1868]).

price of production, cost-price and value

The cost-price of a commodity refers only to the quantity of paid labour contained in it, while its value refers to all the paid and unpaid labour contained in it. The price of production refers to the sum of the paid labour plus a certain quantity of unpaid labour determined for any particular sphere of production by conditions over which it has no control. . . . The cost-price is smaller than the price of production. . . . The cost-price is smaller than the value. . . . In Books I and II we dealt only with the value of commodities. On the one hand, the cost-price has now been singled out as a part of this value, and, on the other, the price of production of commodities has been developed as its converted form.

Suppose the composition of the average social capital is $80_c + 20_v$, and the annual rate of surplus-value, s', is 100%. In that case the average annual profit for a capital of 100 = 20, and the general annual rate of profit = 20%. Whatever the cost-price, k, of the commodities annually produced by a capital of 100, their price of production would then be k + 20. In those spheres of production in which the composition of capital would = $(80 - x)_c + (20 + x)_v$, the actually produced surplus-value, or the annual profit produced in that particular sphere, would be 20 + x, that is, greater than 20, and the value of the produced commodities = k + 20 + x, that is, greater than k + 20, or greater than their price of production. In those spheres, in which the composition of the capital = $(80 + x)_c + (20 - x)_v$, the annually produced surplus-value, or profit, would = 20 - x, or less than 20, and consequently the value of the commodities k + 20 - x less than the price of production, which = k + 20. Aside from possible differences in the periods of turnover, the price of production of the commodities would then equal their value only in spheres, in which the composition would happen to be $80_c + 20_v$. . . . In all shorter periods (quite aside from fluctuations of market-prices), a change in the prices of production is, therefore, always traceable *prima facie* to actual changes in the values of commodities, i.e. to changes in the total amount of labour-time required for their production. Mere changes in the money expression of the same values are, naturally, not at all considered here (*Capital* 3.163–6; Penguin *Capital* 3.263–6).

Price-rises   *See* Speculation.

Primitive accumulation   *See* Accumulation.

Private property   *See* Property, private.

Process

Constant motion, change, transformation, development (*SW* 408 [*Socialism, Utopian and Scientific*, first published 1880 E]).

Process of circulation

Phase of the total process of reproduction. But no value is produced in the process of circulation, and, therefore, no surplus-value (*Capital* 3.279; Penguin *Capital* 3.392).

Process of creating value

If we . . . compare the process of producing value with the labour-process, pure and simple, we find that the latter consists of the useful labour, the work that produces use-values. Here we contemplate the labour as producing a particular article; we view it under its qualitative aspect alone, with regard to its end and aim. But viewed as a value-creating process, the same labour-process presents itself under its quantitative aspect alone (*Capital* 1.190; Penguin *Capital* 1.302). *See also* Realization process.

Process of production

Immediate unity of labour-process and valorization process (Penguin *Capital* 1.991).

Process involving the factors of the labour-process into which the capitalist's money has been converted and which proceeds under his direction with the sole purpose of using money to make more money (Penguin *Capital* 1.1020).

Functioning of the means of production (*Capital* 2.125; Penguin *Capital* 2.200).

As the unity of the labour-process and the formation of value, the process of production is the production of commodities; as the unity of the labour-process and the increase of value it is the capitalist production of commodities (*Werke* 16.263 [*Konspekt über Das Kapital*, written 1868 E]).

capitalist process of production

Sale and purchase of labour-power (Penguin *Capital* 1.1017)

Actual consumption of the labour-power purchased (Penguin *Capital* 1.1017).

If then, on the one hand, the capitalist mode of production presents itself to us historically, as a necessary condition to the transformation of the labour-process into a social process, so, on the other hand, this social form of the labour-process presents itself, as a method employed by capital for the more profitable exploitation of labour, by increasing that labour's productiveness (*Capital* 1.317; Penguin *Capital* 1.453).

Not merely the production of commodities. It is a process which absorbs unpaid labour, which makes raw materials and means of labour – the means of production – into means for the absorption of unpaid labour (*Theories of Surplus Value* 1.401).

Producers (associated) *See* Class; Communism; Freedom; Nationalization.

Production

Action on nature (*CW* 9.211 [note to *Wage Labour and Capital*, first published 1891 E]).

Real wealth (*CW* 7.470 [*Thiers's Speech*, first published 1848]).

The appropriation of nature on the part of the individual within and by means of a determinate form of society (*Texts on Method* 54 [*Introduction to the Grundrisse*, written 1857]).

A certain social body, a social subject, which is active in a greater or lesser totality of branches of production (*Texts on Method* 52 [*Introduction to the Grundrisse*, written 1857]).

Production is immediately also consumption. Consumption is twofold, subjective and objective: Firstly, the individual, who develops his capabilities in producing, expends them as well; he consumes them in the act of production. . . . Secondly: consumption of the means of production, which are used and worn out. . . . It supplies the material, the object. . . . Not only the object of consumption but also the mode of consumption is produced by production. . . . Therefore production creates the consumer (*Texts on Method* 58–61 [*Introduction to the Grundrisse*, written 1857]).

An objectification of the individual (Penguin *Grundrisse* 226).

Development of certain capacities on the part of the subject (Penguin *Grundrisse* 492).

Development of human productive forces (*Theories of Surplus Value* 2.117).

See also Act of production; Cost of production; Elements of production; Instruments of Production; Means of production; Period of production; Price of production; Process of production; Relations of production.

capitalist production

The production of surplus-value, the absorption of surplus-labour (*Capital* 1.253; Penguin *Capital* 1.376).

Mass production from the very outset (*Capital* 3.181; Penguin *Capital* 3.282).

Three cardinal facts of capitalist production:

(1) Concentration of means of production in few hands, whereby they cease to appear as the property of the immediate labourers and turn into social production capacities. Even if initially they are the private property of capitalists. These are the trustees of bourgeois society, but they pocket all the proceeds of their trusteeship.

(2) Organization of labour itself into social labour: through co-operation, division of labour, and the uniting of labour with the natural sciences.

In these two senses, the capitalist mode of production abolishes private property and private labour, even though in contradictory forms.

(3) Creation of the world-market (*Capital* 3.266; Penguin *Capital* 3.375).

Capitalist production begins from the moment when the conditions of labour belong to one class, and another class has at its disposal only labour-power. This separation of labour from the conditions of labour is the precondition of capitalist production (*Theories of Surplus Value* 1.78).

See also Insurance fund; Supervision.

limits on capitalist production

Capitalist production is by no means an absolute form for the development of the productive forces and for the creation of

wealth, but rather that at a certain point it comes into collision with this development. This collision appears partly in
periodical crises, which arise from the circumstance that now
this and now that portion of the labouring population
becomes redundant under its old mode of employment. The
limit of capitalist production is the excess time of the labourers
(*Capital* 3.263-4; Penguin *Capital* 3.372-3).

necessary production
Necessary population – i.e. that which represents necessary
labour, labour necessary for production (Penguin *Grundrisse*
608).

social production
Production of the requirements of life (*Dialectics of Nature* 48
E).

Production-time

The duration of the sojourn in the sphere of production
(*Capital* 2.124; Penguin *Capital* 2.200).
The time of production naturally comprises the period of the
labour-process, but is not comprised in it (*Capital* 2.124;
Penguin *Capital* 2.200).
That time in which a capital produces use-values and
expands, hence functions as productive capital, although it
includes time in which it is either latent or produces without
expanding its value (*Capital* 2.127; Penguin *Capital* 2.203).

production-time of the means of production
The time during which they function as means of production,
hence serve in the productive process (*Capital* 2.125; Penguin
Capital 2.200).
The stops during which the process of production, and thus
the functioning of the means of production embodied in it, are
interrupted (*Capital* 2.125; Penguin *Capital* 2.200).
The time during which they are held in readiness as prerequi-
sites of that process, hence already represent productive
capital but have not yet entered into the process of production
(*Capital* 2.125; Penguin *Capital* 2.200-1).
The time of production of the means of production does not

mean in this case the time required for their production, but the time during which they take part in the process of production of a certain commodity (*Capital* 2.124 E; Penguin *Capital* 2.200 E).

Productive forces

The basis of all men's history (*SC* 35 [to Annenkov, 28 December 1846]).
The result of practical human energy; but this energy is itself conditioned by the circumstances in which men find themselves, by the productive forces already acquired, by the social form which exists before they do, which they do not create, which is the product of the preceding generation (*SC* 35 [to Annenkov, 28 December 1846]).
See also Communism; Free trade; Production; Profit; Relations of production, bourgeois; Revolution; Society, bourgeois; Structure; Wealth.

Productive power

The efficacy of any special productive activity during a given time (*Capital* 1.53; Penguin *Capital* 1.137).
The productive force of society is measured in fixed capital, exists there in its objective form (Penguin *Grundrisse* 694).
See also Crises; Productivity.

determination of productive power

The productiveness of labour is determined by various circumstances amongst others, by the average amount of skill of the workmen, the state of science, and the degree of its practical application, the social organization of production, the extent and capabilities of the means of production, and by physical conditions (*Capital* 1.47; Penguin *Capital* 1.130).

growth of productive power

The growth of the productive power of labour is identical in meaning with (a) the growth of relative surplus value or of the relative surplus labour time which the worker gives to capital; (b) the decline of the labour-time necessary for the reproduction of labour capacity; (c) the decline of the part of capital which exchanges it all for living labour relative to the parts of it which participate in the production process as objectified labour and as presupposed value (Penguin *Grundrisse* 763).

productive power of labour

Relative decrease of variable in relation to constant capital, and consequently to the total capital set in motion (*Capital* 3.212; Penguin *Capital* 3.318).

Progressively higher organic composition of the social capital in its average (*Capital* 3.212; Penguin *Capital* 3.318).

The development of the social productiveness of labour is manifested in two ways: first, in the magnitude of the already produced productive forces, the value and mass of the conditions of production under which new production is carried on, and in the absolute magnitude of the already accumulated productive capital; secondly, in the relative smallness of the portion of total capital laid out in wages. . . . In relation to employed labour-power the development of the productivity again reveals itself in two ways: First, in the increase of surplus-labour, i.e. the reduction of the necessary labour-time required for the reproduction of labour-power. Secondly, in the decrease of the quantity of labour-power (the number of labourers) generally employed to set in motion a given capital (*Capital* 3.247; Penguin *Capital* 3.355).

See Labour, productive, skilled; Natural elements; Productivity; Wealth.

Productivity

Labour-power is productive through the difference between its value and the value which it creates (*Theories of Surplus Value* 1.392).

See also Degree of productivity.

productivity of capital

The productivity of capital consists in the fact that it confronts labour as wage-labour, and the productivity of labour consists in the fact that it confronts the means of labour as capital (*Theories of Surplus Value* 1.394).

The total productivity of capital is = the duration of one production phase multiplied by the number of times it is repeated in a certain period of time. But this number is determined by circulation time (Penguin *Grundrisse* 630).

The productivity of capital as capital is not the productive force which increases use values; but rather its capacity to create value; the degree to which it produces value (Penguin *Grundrisse* 630).

See also Capital, productive.

productivity of labour

An increase in the productivity of labour means nothing more than that the same capital creates the same value with less labour, or that less labour creates the same product with more capital (Penguin *Grundrisse* 388).

The maximum of product with the minimum of work, hence too goods constantly become cheaper (Penguin *Capital* 1.1037).

An alteration in the labour-process of such a kind as to shorten the labour-time socially necessary for the production of a commodity and to endow a given quantity of labour with the power of producing a greater quantity of use-value (*Capital* 1.298; Penguin *Capital* 1.431).

The increasing productivity of labour (insofar as it is connected with machinery) is identical with the decreasing number of workers relatively to the number and extent of the machinery employed (*Theories of Surplus Value* 3.365).

productivity of machines

The productivity of a machine is measured by the point at which it replaces the power of human labour (*Werke* 16.280 [*Konspekt über Das Kapital*, written 1868 E]).

Profit

Rent of land, profit, etc., these actual forms of existence of private property (*CW* 5.231 [*German Ideology*, written 1845–6]).

Deduction from wages (Penguin *Grundrisse* 330).

Only a secondary, derivative and transformed form of surplus value, the bourgeois form, in which the traces of its origin are extinguished (Penguin *Grundrisse* 595).

The sum of surplus value expressed as a proportion of the total value of the capital (Penguin *Grundrisse* 767).

The surplus value, or that part of the total value of the commodity in which the surplus labour or unpaid labour of the working man is realized (*SW* 213 [*Wages, Price and Profit,* written 1865]).

Excess value of a commodity over its cost-price (*Capital* 3.42; Penguin *Capital* 3.133).

The excess of the total labour embodied in the commodity over the paid labour embodied in it (*Capital* 3.42; Penguin *Capital* 3.133).

A converted form of surplus-value, a form in which its origin and the secret of its existence are obscured and extinguished (*Capital* 3.48; Penguin *Capital* 3.139).

An appropriation of national labour (*Capital* 3.542; Penguin *Capital* 3.675).

The main factor, not of the distribution of products, but of their production itself (*Capital* 3.882; Penguin *Capital* 3.1022).

Profit does not result from the exchange of an amount of materialized labour for an equivalent amount of living labour, but from the portion of living labour which is appropriated in this exchange without an equivalent payment in return, that is, from unpaid labour which capital appropriates in this pseudo-exchange (*Theories of Surplus Value* 3.15).

See also Class; Law; Need; Supervision.

average profit

The profit accruing in accordance with this general rate of profit to any capital of a given magnitude, whatever its organic composition (*Capital* 3.158; Penguin *Capital* 3.257).

The total mass of surplus-values allotted to the various quantities of capital proportionally to their magnitudes in the different spheres of production (*Capital* 3.174; Penguin *Capital* 3.274).

A product formed under very definite historical production relations by the movement of social processes, a product which, as we have seen, requires very complex adjustment (*Capital* 3.783; Penguin *Capital* 3.918).

A standard, a regulator of production.

The proportional share of each individual capital in the surplus-value produced by the total social capital (*Capital* 3.783; Penguin *Capital* 3.918).
See also Rate of profit, equalization of.

commercial profit

The excess of the selling price over the price of production of the commodity which, for the merchant, is its purchase price (*Capital* 3.286; Penguin *Capital* 3.399).

determining the average profit

Not by the surplus-labour appropriated at first hand by each capital, but by the quantity of total surplus-labour appropriated by the total capital, from which each individual capital received its dividend only proportional to its aliquot part of the total capital (*Capital* 3.606; Penguin *Capital* 3.742).

equalization of profit

Distribution of the total surplus-value among the various capitals (*Capital* 3.845; Penguin *Capital* 3.985).
See also Rate of profit, equalization of.

gross profit

For the productive capitalist who works on borrowed capital, the gross profit falls into two parts – the interest, which he is to pay the lender, and the surplus over and above the interest, which makes up his own share of the profit (*Capital* 3.372–3; Penguin *Capital* 3.495–6).
The merely quantitative division of the gross profit between two different persons who both have different legal claims to the same capital, and hence to the profit produced by it, thus turns into a qualitative division for both the industrial capitalist in so far as he is operating on borrowed capital, and for the money-capitalist, in so far as he does not himself apply his capital. One portion of the profit appears now as fruit due as such to capital in one form, as interest; the other portion appears as a specific fruit of capital in an opposite form, and thus as profit of enterprise. One appears exclusively as the fruit of operating with the capital, the fruit of performing capital, or of the functions performed by the active capitalist. And this ossification and individualization of the two parts of

the gross profit in respect to one another, as though they originated from two essentially different sources, now takes firm shape for the entire capitalist class and the total capital. And, indeed, regardless of whether the capital employed by the active capitalist is borrowed or not, and whether the capital belonging to the money-capitalist is employed by himself or not. The profit of every capital, and consequently also the average profit established by the equalization of capitals, splits, or is separated, into two qualitatively different, mutually independent and separately individualized parts, to wit – interest and profit of enterprise – both of which are determined by separate laws. The capitalist operating on his own capital, like the one operating on borrowed capital, divides the gross profit into interest due to himself as owner, as his own lender, and into profit of enterprise due to him as to an active capitalist performing his function (*Capital* 3.374–5; Penguin *Capital* 3.498).

The actual value of the total profit (*Capital* 3.373; Penguin *Capital* 3.496).

industrial profit

Excess of the price of production of the commodity over its cost-price (*Capital* 3.286; Penguin *Capital* 3.399).

surplus profit

The difference between the individual price of production of these favoured producers and the general social price of production regulating the market in this entire production sphere. This difference is equal to the excess of the general price of production of the commodities over their individual price of production (*Capital* 3.641; Penguin *Capital* 3.780).

Profit of enterprise

That portion of profit which falls to the active capitalist appears now as profit of enterprise, deriving solely from the operations, or functions, which he performs with the capital in the process of reproduction, hence particularly those functions which he performs as entrepreneur in industry or commerce (*Capital* 3.374; Penguin *Capital* 3.497).

135

Opposite form assumed by the excess of gross profit over interest as soon as this exists as an independent category (*Capital* 3.376; Penguin *Capital* 3.499).
See also Profit, gross.

Proletarians

The man who, being without capital and rent, lives purely by labour (*CW* 3.241 [*Economic and Philosophical Manuscripts*, written 1844]).
In law and in fact, the slave of the bourgeoisie (*CW* 4.376 [*Condition of the Working Class*, first published 1845 E]).
The proletarians in all countries have one and the same interest, one and the same enemy, and one and the same struggle. The great mass of proletarians are, by their very nature, free from national prejudices and their whole disposition and movement is essentially humanitarian, anti-nationalist. Only the proletarians can destroy nationality, only the awakening proletariat can bring about fraternization between the different nations (*CW* 6.6 [*Festival of Nations*, first published 1846 E]).
Product of the great industrial revolution (*First International* 134 [*Prussian Military Question*, first published 1865 E]).
The wage-labourer who produces and increases capital, and is thrown out on the streets as soon as he is superfluous for the needs of aggrandisement of 'Monsieur capital', as Pecqueur calls this person (*Capital* 1.576; Penguin *Capital* 1.764).
Proletarians of all countries, unite! (*First International* 81 [*Inaugural Address*, first published 1864]).

Proletariat

Creation of the world of private property (*CW* 4.35 [*Holy Family*, first-published 1845]).
A really revolutionary class (*CW* 6.494 [*Communist Manifesto*, first published 1848]).
That class of society which procures its means of livelihood entirely and solely from the sale of its labour and not from the profit derived from any capital; whose weal and woe, whose life and death, whose whole existence depends on the demand for labour, hence, on the alternation of times of good and bad

business, on the fluctuations resulting from unbridled competition (*CW* 6.341 [*Principles of Communism*, written 1847 E]).
The class of the proletarians (*CW* 6.343 [*Principles of Communism*, written 1847 E]).
The class of modern wage-labourers, who, having no means of production of their own, are reduced to selling their labour-power in order to live (*CW* 6.482 [note to *Communist Manifesto*, first published 1888 E]).
A class which, owing to its whole position in society, can only free itself by abolishing altogether all class rule, all servitude and all exploitation (*SW* 372 [*Karl Marx*, first published 1878 E]).
The exploited and oppressed class (*SW* 1.24 [Preface to *Communist Manifesto*, first published 1883]).
See Class; Communism; Fraternity; Free trade, and protectionism; Pauperism; Philosophy; Republic; Reserve army; Revolution, total; Workhouses.

agricultural proletariat

That section of the working class which is the last to become aware of its interests and social position and has the most difficulty in understanding them. In other words, it is that section of the working class which remains longest the unconscious tool of an exploiting and privileged class (*First International* 141 [*Prussian Military Question*, first published 1865 E]).

dictatorship of the proletariat

The transition to the abolition of classes (*SW* 1.613 [*Housing Question*, first published 1872–3 E]).
The transition to the abolition of all classes and to a classless society (*SC* 69 [to Weydemeyer, 5 March 1852]).
Every provisional political set-up following a revolution requires a dictatorship, and an energetic dictatorship at that (*CW* 7.431 [*Crisis and Counter-Revolution*, first published 1848]).
The state is not 'abolished'. It withers away (*Anti-Dühring* 333 E).
Between capitalist and communist society lies the period of the revolutionary transformation of the one into the other. Corresponding to this is also a political transition period in which

the state can be nothing but the revolutionary dictatorship of the proletariat (*SW* 327 [*Critique of the Gotha Programme*, written 1875).

In all civilised countries, democracy has as its necessary consequence the political rule of the proletariat, and the political rule of the proletariat is the first condition for all communist measures (*CW* 6.299 [*Communists and Karl Heinzen*, first published 1847 E]).

liberation of the proletariat

Can only be an international action (*Werke* 39.89 [to Paul Lafargue, 27 June 1893 E]).

See also Communism; Free trade; State.

Progress   *See* Development; Division of labour.

Property

The relation of the individual to the natural conditions of labour and of reproduction as belonging to him, as the objective, nature-given inorganic body of his subjectivity (Penguin *Grundrisse* 473).

Property thus originally means no more than a human being's relation to his natural conditions of production as belonging to him, as his, as presupposed along with his own being; relations to them as natural presuppositions of his self, which only form, so to speak, his extended body. . . . Property, in so far as it is only the conscious relation – and posited in regard to the individual by the community, and proclaimed and guaranteed as law – to the conditions of production as his own, so that the producer's being appears also in the objective conditions belonging to him – is only realized by production itself. The real appropriation takes place not in the mental but in the real, active relation to these conditions – in their real positing as the conditions of his subjective activity (Penguin *Grundrisse* 491–3).

Property seemed to us to be based on a man's own labour. . . . Now property turns out to be the right, on the part of the capitalist, to appropriate the unpaid labour of others or its

product, and the impossibility, on the part of the labourer, of appropriating his own product (*Anti-Dühring* 195 E).
See also Capital; City; Tribal property.

individual property *See* Negation, of the negation.

landed property

The first form of private property (*CW* 3.293 [*Economic and Philosophical Manuscripts*, written 1844]).
See also Accumulation, primitive; City; Supervision.

modern bourgeois private property

The final and most complete expression of the system of producing and appropriating products, that is based on class antagonisms, on the exploitation of the many by the few (*CW* 6.498 [*Communist Manifesto*, first published 1848]).

positive supersession of private property

The perceptible appropriation for and by man of the human essence and of human life, of objective man, of human achievements should not be conceived merely in the sense of immediate, one-sided enjoyment, merely in the sense of possessing, of having. Man appropriates his comprehensive essence in a comprehensive manner, that is to say, as a whole man (*CW* 3.299 [*Economic and Philosophical Manuscripts*, written 1844]).
Complete emancipation of all human senses and qualities, but it is this emancipation precisely because these senses and attributes have become, subjectively and objectively, human (*CW* 3.300 [*Economic and Philosophical Manuscripts*, written 1844]).
See also Communism.

private property

The totality of the bourgeois relations of production (*CW* 6.337 [*Moralising Criticism*, first published 1847]).
Means by which labour alienates itself, the realization of this alienation (*CW* 3.280 [*Economic and Philosophical Manuscripts*, written 1844]).
Private property, as the material, summary expression of alienated labour, embraces both relations – the relation of the

worker to labour and to the product of his labour and to the non-worker, and the relation of the non-worker to the worker and to the product of his labour (*CW* 3.281 [*Economic and Philosophical Manuscripts*, written 1844]).

See also Accumulation, primitive; City; Communism; Division of labour; Marriage; Production, capitalist; Proletariat; State; Stock exchange.

Protectionism *See* Free trade.

R

Radical

To be radical is to grasp the root of the matter. But for man the root is man himself (*CW* 3.182 [*Introduction to Critique of Hegel's Philosophy of Law*, first published 1844]).

Radicalism

Pale shadow of early French socialism (*Werke* 36.509 [to Bebel, 18 August 1886 E]).

Rate of interest

If the rate of profit is given, then the relative level of the rate of interest depends on the ratio in which profit is divided between interest and industrial profit. If the ratio of this division is given, then the absolute level of the rate of interest (that is, the ratio of interest to capital) depends on the rate of profit (*Theories of Surplus Value* 3.471).

Rate of profit

The rate of surplus-value measured against the variable capital (*Capital* 3.43; Penguin *Capital* 3.133).
The goad of capitalist production (*Capital* 3.241; Penguin *Capital* 3.349).
Relative increment of capital (*Capital* 3.259; Penguin *Capital* 3.368).
The rate of profit within the production process itself does not depend on surplus-value alone, but also on many other circumstances, such as purchase prices of means of production, methods more productive than the average, on savings of constant capital etc. (*Capital* 3.373; Penguin *Capital* 3.496–7).

determining the general rate of profit

The general rate of profit is, therefore, determined by two factors:

(1) The organic composition of the capitals in the different spheres of production, and thus, the different rates of profit in the individual spheres.

(2) The distribution of the total social capital in these different spheres, and thus, the relative magnitude of the capital invested in each particular sphere at the specific rate of profit prevailing in it, i.e. the relative share of the total social capital absorbed by each individual sphere of production (*Capital* 3.163; Penguin *Capital* 3.263).

determining the rate of profit

The rate of profit, therefore, depends on two main factors – the rate of surplus-value and the value-composition of capital (*Capital* 3.69; Penguin *Capital* 3.161).

equalization of the rate of profit

If commodities are sold at their values, then . . . very different rates of profit arise in the various spheres of production, depending on the different organic composition of the masses of capital invested in them. But capital withdraws from a sphere with a low rate of profit and invades others, which yield a higher profit. Through this incessant outflow and influx, or, briefly, through its distribution among the various spheres, which depends on how the rate of profit falls here and rises there, it creates such a ratio of supply to demand that the average profit in the various spheres of production becomes the same, and values are, therefore, converted into prices of production. Capital succeeds in this equalization, to a greater or lesser degree, depending on the extent of capitalist development in the given nation; i.e. on the extent the conditions in the country in question are adapted for the capitalist mode of production. With the progress of capitalist production, it also develops its own conditions and subordinates to its specific character and its immanent laws all the social prerequisites on which the production process is based (*Capital* 3.195–6; Penguin *Capital* 3.297–8).

falling rate of profit   *See* Law.

general rate of profit
Average of all the different rates of profit (*Capital* 3.158; Penguin *Capital* 3.257).

necessary rate of profit
The rate of profit independent of the movements of competition (*Capital* 3.865; Penguin *Capital* 3.1005).

Rate of rent

$$\frac{\text{Total rental}}{\text{Capital invested}}$$ (*Capital* 3.665; Penguin *Capital* 3.803).

Raw material

The subject of labour has, so to say, been filtered through previous labour. . . . All raw material is the subject of labour, but not every subject of labour is raw material: it can only become so, after it has undergone some alteration by means of labour (*Capital* 1.174; Penguin *Capital* 1.284-5).
See also Conditions of labour; Means of production.

Realization (of capital)

To maintain and to multiply itself as value (Penguin *Grundrisse* 403).
See also Productivity.

Realization process

Essentially the production of surplus-value, i.e. the objectification of unpaid labour (Penguin *Capital* 1.991).

expansion (of capital) and the labour process
In the actual process, the worker uses the means of labour as his tools, and he uses up the object of labour in the sense that it is the material in which his labour manifests itself. It is by this means that he transforms the means of production into the appropriate form of the product. The situation looks quite different in the valorization process. Here it is not the worker

143

who makes use of the means of production, but the means of production that make use of the worker. Living labour does not realize itself in objective labour which thereby becomes its objective organ, but instead objective labour maintains and fortifies itself by drawing off living labour; it is thus that it becomes *value valorizing itself, capital* and functions as such (Penguin *Capital* 1.988).

expansion (of capital) and the production of value

The process of creating surplus-value is nothing but the continuation of the process of producing value beyond a definite point. If on the one hand the process be not carried beyond the point, where the value paid by the capitalist for the labour-power is replaced by an exact equivalent, it is simply a process of producing value; if, on the other hand, it be continued beyond that point, it becomes a process of creating surplus-value (*Capital* 1.189–90; Penguin *Capital* 1.302).

Real wage   *See* Wage.

Reduction   *See* Abstraction; Labour, skilled.

Relations

Our relations in society have to some extent already begun to be established before we are in a position to determine them (*CW* 1.4 [*Reflections*, written 1835]).

economic relations

The material foundation of the present class struggles and national struggles (*CW* 9.197 [*Wage Labour and Capital*, first published 1849]).

Mode in which men in a particular society produce their livelihood and exchange products amongst themselves (as far as the division of labour permits). Hence the whole technology of production and transport is included.

This technology also determines the mode of exchange and the distribution of products and hence after the dissolution of tribal society, the division of society into classes, relations of domination and servitude, hence the state, politics, law etc.

Included in this also are the geographical basis on which these activities take place and the residue of earlier economic developments which persist, often only through tradition or inertia, and of course the milieu surrounding this social form (*Werke* 39.205 [to Borgius, 25 January 1894 E]).

Determining basis of the history of society (*Werke* 39.205 [to Borgius, 25 January 1894 E]).

See also Commerce; Profit; Relations of circulation; Relations of distribution; Relations of production.

material relations *See* History, social.

relations (international)

The expression of a particular division of labour (*SC* 37 [to Annenkov, 28 December 1846]).

Relations of circulation

The characteristic (1) of the product as a commodity, and (2) of the commodity as a product of capital, already implies all circulation relations, i.e. a definite social process through which the products must pass and in which they assume definite social characteristics (*Capital* 3.880; Penguin *Capital* 3.1020).

Relations of distribution

The basis of special social functions performed within the production relations by certain of their agents, as opposed to the direct producers. They imbue the conditions of production themselves and their representatives with a specific social quality. They determine the entire character and the entire movement of production (*Capital* 3.879; Penguin *Capital* 3.1019).

Correspond to and arise from historically determined specific social forms of the process of production and mutual relations entered into by men in the reproduction process of human life (*Capital* 3.883; Penguin *Capital* 3.1023).

The specific historical form of their corresponding production relations (*Capital* 3.884; Penguin *Capital* 3.1024).

Relations of production

Social relations within which individuals produce (*CW* 9.212 [*Wage Labour and Capital*, first published 1849]).

The relations of production in their totality constitute what are called the social relations, society (*CW* 9.212 [*Wage Labour and Capital*, first published 1849]).

Relations which human beings enter into during the process of social life, in the creation of their social life (*Capital* 3.878; Penguin *Capital* 3.1018).

See also Category; Circulation; Communism; Economics; Labour, productive; Money; Revolution; Structure.

bourgeois relations of production

The last antagonistic form of the social process of production – antagonistic not in the sense of individual antagonism, but of one arising from the social conditions of life of the individuals; at the same time the productive forces developing in the womb of bourgeois society create the material conditions for the solution of that antagonism. This social formation brings, therefore, the prehistory of human society to a close (*SW*182 [Preface to *Contribution to Critique of Political Economy*, first published 1859]).

See also Consciousness; Relations; State.

material relations of production *See* History, social.

Religion

The recognition of man in a roundabout way, through an intermediary (*CW* 3.152 [*On the Jewish Question*, first published 1844]).

The self-consciousness and self-esteem of man who has either not yet found himself or has already lost himself again (*CW* 3.175 [*Introduction to Critique of Hegel's Philosophy of Law*, first published 1844]).

Religion is the general theory of that world, its encyclopaedic compedium, its logic in a popular form, its spirtualistic point d'honneur, its enthusiasm, its moral sanction, its solemn complement, its universal source of consolation and justification. It is the fantastic realization of the human essence because the

146

human essence has no true reality. The struggle against religion is therefore indirectly a fight against the world of which religion is the spiritual aroma (*CW* 3.175 [*Introduction to Critique of Hegel's Philosophy of Law*, first published 1844]).

Religion is the sigh of the oppressed creature, the heart of a heartless world, just as it is the spirit of spiritless conditions. It is the opium of the people (*CW* 3.175 [*Introduction to Critique of Hegel's Philosophy of Law*, first published 1844]).

The illusory sun which revolves round man as long as he does not revolve round himself (*CW* 3.176 [*Introduction to Critique of Hegel's Philosophy of Law*, first published 1844]).

The fantastic reflection of human things in the human mind (*Dialectics of Nature* 238 E).

The fantastic reflection in men's minds of these external forces which control their daily life, a reflection in which the terrestrial forces assume the form of supernatural forces (*Anti-Dühring* 374 E).

See also Security.

Rent

A form of surplus-profit, which constitutes its substance (*Capital* 3.675; Penguin *Capital* 3.813).

A surplus over the average profit (*Capital* 3.783; Penguin *Capital* 3.918).

The price paid to the owner of natural forces or mere products of nature for the right of using those forces or appropriating (by labour) those products (*Theories of Surplus Value* 2.247).

See also Profit.

absolute rent

Independent of the differences in fertility of various soil types and in successive investments of capital on the same land (*Capital* 3.760; Penguin *Capital* 3.894–5).

The excess of value over the average price of raw produce (*Theories of Surplus Value* 2.142).

Equal to the difference between individual value and cost-price (*Theories of Surplus Value* 2.293).

agricultural rent

Rent of land which supplies the chief vegetable foods (*Theories of Surplus Value* 2.241).

differential rent

Formal transformation of surplus-profit into rent (*Capital* 3.737; Penguin *Capital* 3.870).

The excess of the market-price of the produce grown on favoured soils over the value of their own produce (*Theories of Surplus Value* 2.142).

The difference in the magnitude of rent – the greater or smaller rent which is due to the different fertility of the various types of land (*Theories of Surplus Value* 2.240).

Does not enter as a determining factor into the general production price of commodities, but rather is based on it. It invariably arises from the difference between the individual production price of a particular capital having command over the monopolized natural force, on the one hand, and the general production price of the total capital invested in the sphere of production concerned, on the other (*Capital* 3.646; Penguin *Capital* 3.785).

Does not arise from the absolute increase in the productiveness of employed capital, or labour appropriated by it, since this can only reduce the value of commodities; it is due to the greater relative fruitfulness of specific separate capitals invested in a certain production sphere, as compared with investments of capital which are excluded from these exceptional and natural conditions favouring productiveness (*Capital* 3.646; Penguin *Capital* 3.785).

Equal to the difference between market-value and individual value (*Theories of Surplus Value* 2.293).

See also Value.

ground-rent

The independent and specific form of landed property on the basis of the capitalist mode of production (*Capital* 3.624; Penguin *Capital* 3.762).

Surplus-value, the product of surplus-labour. In its undeveloped form as rent in kind it is still directly the surplus-product itself (*Capital* 3.634; Penguin *Capital* 3.772–3).

labour-rent

The simplest and most primitive form of rent. Rent is here the primeval form of surplus-labour and coincides with it (*Capital* 3.792; Penguin *Capital* 3.928).

money-rent

By money rent – as distinct from industrial and commercial ground-rent based upon the capitalist mode of production, which is but an excess over average profit – we here mean the ground-rent which arises from a mere change in form of rent in kind (*Capital* 3.796; Penguin *Capital* 3.932).

rate of differential rent

The ratio of that portion of surplus-value converted into rent to the invested capital which produces the agricultural product. This differs from the ratio of surplus-product to total product, for the total product does not comprise the entire invested capital, namely, the fixed capital, which continues to exist alongside the product. On the other hand, it covers the fact that on soils yielding differential rent an increasing portion of the product is transformed into an excess of surplus-product (*Capital* 3.777; Penguin *Capital* 3.912).

Replacement (of consumed capital)

Replacement of values represented by certain means of production (*Capital* 3.745; Penguin *Capital* 3.879).

Replacement costs   *See* Cost of circulation; Unproductive costs.

Reproduction

Appropriation of the objects by the subjects; formation, subjugation of the objects to a subjective purpose; their transformation into results and repositories of subjective activity (Penguin *Grundrisse* 489).
Means of reproducing as capital – i.e. as self-expanding value – the value advanced.
. To go on producing (*Capital* 1.531; Penguin *Capital* 1.711).
Does not result from accumulation – transformation of

149

surplus-value into capital – but from the reconversion of the value which has branched off, detached itself in the form of money from the body of the fixed capital into new additional or at least more effective fixed capital of the same kind (*Capital* 2.175; Penguin *Capital* 2.251).

Extensive if the field of production is extended; intensive if the means of production is made more effective (*Capital* 2.175; Penguin *Capital* 2.251).

simple reproduction

Actual factor of accumulation (*Capital* 2.399; Penguin *Capital* 2.471).

Material substratum of extended reproduction (*Capital* 2.501; Penguin *Capital* 2.573).

Reproduction-period

The time during which the instrument of labour wears out and must be replaced by another of the same kind (*Capital* 2.166; Penguin *Capital* 2.243).

Reproduction process

The direct process of the production of capital is its labour and self-expansion process, the process whose result is the commodity-product and whose compelling motive is the production of surplus-value.

The process of reproduction of capital comprises this direct process of production as well as the two phases of the circulation process proper, i.e. the entire circuit which, as a periodic process – a process which constantly repeats itself in definite periods – constitutes the turnover of capital (*Capital* 2.355; Penguin *Capital* 2.427).

See also Crises.

Republic (democratic)

Specific form for the dictatorship of the proletariat (*Werke* 22.235 [*Zur Kritik des S-D Programmentwurfs*, written 1891 E]).

The one political form in which the battle between the working class and the capitalist class can assume a general

character and then be completed with the decisive victory of the proletariat (*Werke* 22.280 [*Antwort an G. Bovio*, first published 1892 E].
The last form of bourgeois rule, that in which it goes to pieces (*SC* 371 [to Bernstein, 24 March 1884]).
See also Ideology.

Reserve army

industrial reserve army

But if a surplus labouring population is a necessary product of accumulation or of the development of wealth on a capitalist basis, this surplus-population becomes, conversely, the lever of capitalistic accumulation, nay, a condition of existence of the capitalist mode of production. It forms a disposable industrial reserve army, that belongs to capital quite as absolutely as if the latter had bred it at its own cost. Independently of the limits of the actual increase of population, it creates, for the changing needs of the self-expansion of capital, a mass of human material always ready for exploitation (*Capital* 1.592; Penguin *Capital* 1.784).

Reserve fund

Not a constituent part of capital already performing its functions, or, to be more exact, of money-capital. It is rather a part of capital in a preliminary stage of its accumulation, of surplus-value not yet transformed into active capital (*Capital* 2.87; Penguin *Capital* 2.165).

Revenue

The part of surplus-value destined for immediate consumption (Penguin *Grundrisse* 733).
Part of the value of commodity-capital transformed into money (*Capital* 3.503; Penguin *Capital* 3.636).
An expression and result of actual accumulation (*Capital* 3.503; Penguin *Capital* 3.636).
The word revenue is used in a double sense: first, to designate surplus-value so far as it is the fruit periodically yielded by

capital; secondly, to designate the part of that fruit which is periodically consumed by the capitalist, or added to the fund that supplies his private consumption. I have retained this double meaning because it harmonizes with the language of the English and French economists (*Capital* 1.554; Penguin *Capital* 1.738).

Revolution

A purely natural phenomenon which is guided more according to physical laws than by the rules which in ordinary times determine the development of society. Or rather these rules assume in revolutionary times a much more physical character, the material force of necessity appears more strongly (*Werke* 27.190 [to Marx, 13 February 1851 E]).

The act whereby one part of the population imposes its will upon the other party by means of rifles, bayonets and cannon – authoritarian means (*SW* 1.639 [*On Authority*, first published 1874 E]).

Long, drawn out process (MEW 36.38 [to Bernstein, 12–13 June 1883 E]).

Not criticism but revolution is the driving force of history (*CW* 5.54 [*German Ideology*, written 1845–6]).

See also Communism; Emancipation; Free trade; Stock exchange.

communist revolution

The most radical rupture with traditional property relations (*CW* 6.504 [*Communist Manifesto*, first published 1848]).

people's revolution

If you look at the last chapter of my *Eighteenth Brumaire*, you will find that I declare that the next attempt of the French Revolution will be no longer, as before, to transfer the bureaucratic-military machine from one hand to another, but to smash it, and this is the preliminary condition for every real people's revolution on the Continent (*SC* 262–3 [to Kugelmann, 12 April 1871]).

proletarian revolution

Resolution of contradictions (*Werke* 20.620 [*Ergänzungen Anti-Dühring* E]).

revolutions of 1648 and 1789

The revolutions of 1648 and 1789 were not English and French revolutions, they were revolutions of a European type. They did not represent the victory of a particular class of society over the old political order; they proclaimed the political order of the new European society. The bourgeoisie was victorious in these revolutions, but the victory of the bourgeoisie was at that time the victory of a new social order, the victory of bourgeois ownership over feudal ownership, of nationality over provincialism, of competition over the guild, of the division of land over primogeniture, of the rule of the landowner over the domination of the owner by the land, of enlightenment over superstition, of the family over the family name, of industry over heroic idleness, of bourgeois law over medieval privileges (*CW* 8.161 [*Bourgeoisie and Counter-Revolution*, first published 1848]).

revolutions of February and June 1848

The February revolution was the nice revolution, the revolution of universal sympathies, because the contradictions which erupted in it against the monarchy were still under-developed and peacefully dormant, because the social struggle which formed their background had only achieved a nebulous existence, an existence in phrases, in words. The June revolution is the ugly revolution, the nasty revolution, because the phrases have given place to the real thing, because the republic has bared the head of the monster by knocking off the crown which shielded and concealed it (*CW* 7.147 [*June Revolution*, first published 1848]).

The June revolution is the revolution of despair and is fought with silent anger and the gloomy cold-bloodedness of despair. The workers know that they are involved in a fight to the death and in the face of the battle's terrible seriousness, even the cheerful French *esprit* remains silent. . . . The June revolution is the first which has actually divided all society into two large hostile armed camps which are represented by Eastern

Paris and Western Paris. The unanimity of the February revolution, that poetic unanimity full of dazzling delusions and
beautiful lies so appropriately symbolised by that windbag
and traitor Lamartine, has disappeared (*CW* 7.130–1 [*23rd of
June*, first published 1848 E]).

social revolution

At a certain stage of their development, the material productive forces of society come in conflict with the existing
relations of production, or – what is but a legal expression for
the same thing – with the property relations within which
they have been at work hitherto. From forms of development
of the productive forces these relations turn into their fetters.
Then begins an epoch of social revolution. With the change of
the economic foundation the entire immense superstructure is
more or less rapidly transformed. In considering such trans-
formations a distinction should always be made between the
material transformation of the economic conditions of production, which can be determined with the precision of
natural science, and the legal, political, religious, aesthetic or
philosophic – in short, ideological forms in which men become
conscious of this conflict and fight it out. Just as our opinion of
an individual is not based on what he thinks of himself, so can
we not judge of such a period of transformation by its own
consciousness; on the contrary, this consciousness must be
explained rather from the contradictions of material life, from
the existing conflict between the social productive forces and
the relations of production. No social order ever perishes
before all the productive forces for which there is room in it
have developed; and new, higher relations of production
never appear before the material conditions of their existence
have matured in the womb of the old society itself. Therefore
mankind always sets itself only such tasks as it can solve; since,
looking at the matter more closely, it will always be found
that the task itself arises only when the material conditions for
its solution already exist or are at least in the process of formation (*SW* 181–2 [Preface to *Contribution to Critique of Political
Economy*, first published 1859]).

total revolution

The antagonism between the proletariat and the bourgeoisie is a struggle of class against class, a struggle which carried to its highest expression is a total revolution. Indeed, is it at all surprising that a society founded on the opposition of classes should culminate in brutal contradiction, the shock of body against body, as its final denouement? (*CW* 6.212 [*Poverty of Philosophy*, first published 1847]).

universal revolution

Will it be possible for this revolution to take place in one country alone?

No. Large-scale industry, already by creating the world market, has so linked up all the peoples of the earth, and especially the civilized peoples, that each people is dependent on what happens to another. Further, in all civilized countries large-scale industry has so levelled social development that in all these countries the bourgeoisie and the proletariat have become the two decisive classes of society and the struggle between them the main struggle of the day. The communist revolution will therefore be no merely national one; it will be a revolution taking place simultaneously in all civilized countries, that is, at least in England, America, France and Germany. In each of these countries it will develop more quickly or more slowly according to whether the country has a more developed industry, more wealth, and a more considerable mass of productive forces. It will therefore be slowest and most difficult to carry out in Germany, quickest and easiest in England. It will also have an important effect upon the other countries of the world, and will completely change and greatly accelerate their previous manner of development. It is a worldwide revolution and will therefore be worldwide in scope (*CW* 6.351–2 [*Principles of Communism*, written 1847 E]).

S

Savings banks

The golden chain by which the government holds a large part
of the working class (*CW* 6.427 [*Wages*, written 1847]).
See also Bank.

Science

A product of man's own practical activity (*CW* 3.322
[*Economic and Philosophical Manuscripts*, written 1844]).
Natural science will in time incorporate into itself the science
of man, just as the science of man will incorporate into itself
natural science; there will be one science (*CW* 3.304 [*Economic
and Philosophical Manuscripts*, written 1844]).
Productive force generally (Penguin *Grundrisse* 694).
General product of social development (Penguin *Capital*
1.1024).
Historically effective revolutionary force (*Werke* 19.336
[*Begräbnis von Karl Marx*, first published 1883 E]).

Security

Security is the highest social concept of civil society, the
concept of police, expressing the fact that the whole of society
exists only in order to guarantee to each of its members the
preservation of his person, his rights, and his property. . . .
The concept of security does not raise civil society above its
egoism. On the contrary, security is the insurance of its egoism
(*CW* 3.163–4 [*On the Jewish Question*, first published 1844]).
See also Property.

Self-consciousness   *See* Consciousness; Equality.

Self-expansion of value

Self-expansion of capital
The creation of surplus-value (Penguin *Capital* 1.990).
The determining, dominating and overriding purpose of the capitalist; the absolute motive and content of his activity (Penguin *Capital* 1.990).

Self-sacrifice
In definite circumstances a necessary form of the self-assertion of individuals (*CW* 5.247 [*German Ideology*, written 1845–6]).

Sensuous
To be sensuous is to suffer (*CW* 3.337 [*Economic and Philosophical Manuscripts*, written 1844]).
See also Consciousness; Materialism.

Sensuousness *See* Science.

Serfs *See* Proletarians.

emancipation of the serfs
Excuse for a new division of estates between the nobility and the kulaks (*Werke* 22.534 [*Interview*, first published 1892 E]).

Service
Useful effect of a use-value, be it of a commodity, or be it of labour (*Capital* 1.187; Penguin *Capital* 1.299–300).
An expression for the particular use-value of labour where the latter is useful not as an article, but as an activity (*Capital* 1.1047).
Where the direct exchange of money for labour takes place without the latter producing capital, where it is therefore not productive labour, it is bought as service, which in general is nothing but a term for the particular use-value which the labour provides, like any other commodity; it is however a specific term for the particular use-value of labour in so far as

157

it does not render service in the form of a thing, but in the form of an activity (*Theories of Surplus Value* 1.403–4).

Shares

A share of stock is merely a title of ownership to a corresponding portion of the surplus-value to be realized by it (*Capital* 3.466; Penguin *Capital* 3.597).
Spheres of investment for loanable capital – capital intended for bearing interest. They are forms of loaning such capital. But they themselves are not the loan capital, which is invested in them. (*Capital* 3.478; Penguin *Capital* 3.609).
Those which are not fakes are titles of ownership of some corporative real capital and drafts on the surplus-value accruing annually from it (*Capital* 2.353; Penguin *Capital* 2.423).
See also Supervision.

Silver *See* Gold.

Sinking fund

The fund for wear and tear of the fixed capital (*Theories of Surplus Value* 3.59).

Slave *See* Proletarian.

Slavery

An economic category of the highest importance (*SC* 41 [to Annenkov, 28 December 1846]).
The dominant form of production among all peoples who were developing beyond the old community, but in the end it was also one of the chief causes of their decay (*Anti-Dühring* 216 E).
Forms of bondage and class domination (*Anti-Dühring* 218 E).
The simplest and most natural form of the division of labour between the masses discharging simple manual labour and the few privileged person directing labour, conducting trade and

public affairs, and, at a later stage, occupying themselves with art and science (*Anti-Dühring* 217 E).
See also Accumulation, primitive.

Social capital

The capital, which in itself rests on a social mode of production and presupposes a social concentration of means of production and labour-power, is here directly endowed with the form of social capital (capital of directly associated individuals) as distinct from private capital, and its undertakings assume the form of social undertakings as distinct from private undertakings. It is the abolition of capital as private property within the framework of capitalist production itself (*Capital* 3.436; Penguin *Capital* 3.567).
See also Centralization; Composition, of capital.

Social formation   *See* Loan capital; Merchant capital; Productive forces; Relations of production, bourgeois; Society.

Socialism

Not merely a local but an international problem which must be resolved through international action by workers (*Werke* 34.511 [*Interview*, first published 1878]).
Socialism of all shades: socialism conscious and unconscious, socialism prosaic and poetic, socialism of the working class and of the middle class, for, verily, that abomination of abominations, socialism, has not only become respectable, but has actually donned evening dress and lounges lazily on drawing-room *causeuses* (*SW* 2.417 [Preface, *Condition of the Working Class*, first published 1892 E]).

modern socialism

In its essence, the direct product of the recognition, on the one hand, of the class antagonisms existing in the society of today between proprietors and non-proprietors, between capitalists and wage-workers; on the other hand, of the anarchy existing in production (*Anti-Dühring* 25 E).

In its theoretical form, modern socialism originally appears ostensibly as a more logical extension of the principles laid down by the great French philosophers of the eighteenth century (*Anti-Dühring* 25 E).
See also Communism.

state socialism

This term does not express a clear concept at all but is a mere journalistic expression like 'the social question' etc., purely a phrase with which one can mean everything and nothing. Disputing the real meaning of such a term is no earthly use to anybody; its real meaning is that it does not have one (*Werke* 38.511 [to Bebel, 6 November 1892 E]).

Society

The complete unity of man with nature – the true resurrection of nature – the accomplished naturalism of man and the accomplished humanism of nature (*CW* 3.298 [*Economic and Philosophical Manuscripts*, written 1844]).
The product of men's reciprocal action (*SC* 35 [to Annenkov, 28 December 1846]).
The relations of production in their totality (*CW* 9.212 [*Wage Labour and Capital*, first published 1849]).
The human being itself in its social relations (Penguin *Grundrisse* 712).
No solid crystal, but an organism capable of change, and is constantly changing (*Capital* 1.21; Penguin *Capital* 1.93).
The aggregate of these relations, in which the agents of this production stand with respect to Nature and to one another, and in which they produce, is precisely society, considered from the standpoint of its economic structure (*Capital* 3.818; Penguin *Capital* 3.957).
See also Class; Dialectic; Economy; Money; Nationalization; Need; Rate of profit, equalization of; Structure (economic).

bourgeois society

War against one another of all individuals, who are no longer isolated from one another by anything but their individuality, and the universal unrestrained movement of the elementary forces of life freed from the fetters of privilege (*CW* 4.116 [*Holy Family*, first published 1845]).

Civil [or bourgeois] society embraces the whole material intercourse of individuals within a definite stage of the development of productive forces. It embraces the whole commercial and industrial life of a given stage and, insofar, transcends the state and the nation, though, on the other hand again, it must assert itself in its external relations as nationality and internally must organize itself as state. The term 'civil society' emerged in the eighteenth century, when property relations had already extricated themselves from the ancient and medieval community. Civil society as such only develops with the bourgeoisie; the social organisation evolving directly out of production and intercourse, which in all ages forms the basis of the state and of the rest of the idealistic superstructure, has, however, always been designated by the same name (*CW* 5.89 [*German Ideology*, written 1845–6]).

Phase of social development in which the Bourgeoisie, the Middle Class, the class of industrial and commercial Capitalists, is, socially and politically, the ruling class; which is now the case more or less in all the civilized countries of Europe and America. By the expressions: Bourgeois society, and: industrial and commercial society, we therefore propose to designate the same stage of social development; the first expression referring, however, more to the fact of the middle class being the ruling class, in opposition either to the class whose rule it superseded (the feudal nobility), or to those classes which it succeeds in keeping under its social and political dominion (the proletariat or industrial working class, the rural population etc.) – while the designation of commercial and industrial society more particularly bears upon the mode of production and distribution characteristic of this phase of social history (*Werke* 28.139 [to Marx, 23 September 1852 E]).

The most developed and most diverse historical organization of production (*Texts on Method* 78 [*Introduction to the Grundrisse*, written 1857]).

Antithetical form of development (*Texts on Method* 79 [*Introduction to the Grundrisse*, written 1857]).

See also Bureaucracy; Emancipation, political; Revolution; Security; Stock exchange.

Species   *See* Life.

Species-being

The animal is immediately one with its life activity. It does not distinguish itself from it. It is its life activity. Man makes his life activity itself the object of his will and of his consciousness. He has conscious life activity. It is not a determination with which he directly merges. Conscious life activity distinguishes man immediately from animal life activity. It is just because of this that he is a species-being (*CW* 3.276 [*Economic and Philosophical Manuscripts*, written 1844]).

In creating a world of objects by his practical activity, in his work upon inorganic nature, man proves himself a conscious species-being, i.e. as a being that treats the species as its own essential being, or that treats itself as a species-being (*CW* 3.276 [*Economic and Philosophical Manuscripts*, written 1844]).

See also Death; Division of labour; Emancipation, human; Equality.

Speculation

Cause of rise in prices (*Capital* 3.422; Penguin *Capital* 3.552).

over-speculation

Symptom of over-production (*CW* 10.490 [*May to October*, written 1850]).

Spirit   *See* Mind.

State

The intermediary between man and man's freedom (*CW* 3.152 [*On the Jewish Question*, first published 1844]).

The system of society (*CW* 3.197 [*Critical Notes*, first published 1844]).

Form of organization which the bourgeois are compelled to adopt, both for internal and external purposes, for the mutual guarantee of their property and interests (*CW* 5.90 [*German Ideology*, written 1845–6]).

The form in which the individuals of a ruling class assert their common interests, and in which the whole civil society of an epoch is epitomised (*CW* 5.90 [*German Ideology,* written 1845–6]).

The ruling class establishes its joint domination as public power, as the state (*CW* 5.355 [*German Ideology,* written 1845–6]).

Organized power of one class for oppressing another (*CW* 6.505 [*Communist Manifesto,* first published 1848]).

By making its burial place the birthplace of the bourgeois republic, the proletariat compelled the latter to come out forthwith in its pure form as the state whose admitted object it is to perpetuate the rule of capital, the slavery of labour (*CW* 10.69 [*Class Struggles in France,* first published 1850]).

Supernaturalist abortion of society (*Paris Commune* 150 [first draft, *Civil War in France,* written 1871]).

Centralized and organized governmental power (*Paris Commune* 151 [first draft, *Civil War in France,* written 1871]).

Organized and collective power of the possessing classes, the landowners and the capitalists, as against the exploited classes, the peasants and the workers (*SW* 1.604 [*Housing Question,* first published 1872–3 E]).

Organization that bourgeois society takes on in order to support the general external conditions of the capitalist mode of production against the encroachments as well of the workers as of individual capitalists (*Anti-Dühring* 330 E).

Essentially a capitalist machine, the state of the capitalists (*Anti-Dühring* 330 E).

Force in its organized form (*Werke* 20.590 [*Materialien Anti-Dühring* E]).

An independent power *vis-à-vis* society (*SW* 617 [*Ludwig Feuerbach,* first published 1886 E]).

Nothing but a machine for the oppression of one class by another (*SW* 258 [*Introduction to Civil War in France,* first published 1891 E]).

See also Bureaucracy; Commune; Elections; International; Nationalization; Proletariat, dictatorship of; Relations, economic; Society, bourgeois; State power; Tariffs; Taxes; Town.

abolition of the state

Has meaning with the communists only as the necessary consequence of the abolition of classes with which the need for the organized might of one class to keep the others down automatically disappears (*CW* 10.333 [review, de Girardin, first published 1850]).

The modern state, again, is only the organization that bourgeois society takes on in order to support the general external conditions of the capitalist mode of production against the encroachments as well of the workers as of individual capitalists. The modern state, no matter what its form, is essentially a capitalist machine, the state of the capitalists, the ideal personification of the total national capital. The more it proceeds to the taking over of the productive forces, the more does it actually become the national capitalist, the more citizens does it exploit. The workers remain wage-workers – proletarians. The capitalist relation is not done away with. It is rather brought to a head. But, brought to a head, it topples over. State ownership of the productive forces is not the solution of the conflict, but concealed within it are the technical conditions that form the elements of that solution. . . . While the capitalist mode of production forces on more and more the transformation of the vast means of production, already socialized, into state property, it shows itself the way to accomplishing this revolution. The proletariat seizes political power and turns the means of production in the first instance into state property. But in doing this it abolishes itself as proletariat, abolishes all class distinctions and class antagonisms, abolishes also the state as state. . . . The state is not 'abolished'. It withers away (*Anti-Dühring* 330–3 E).

See also Proletariat, dictatorship of.

basis of the state   *See* Law.

bourgeois state

Mutual insurance of the bourgeois class against its individual members, as well as against the exploited class, insurance which will necessarily become increasingly expensive and to all appearances increasingly independent of bourgeois society, because the oppression of the exploited class is becoming ever more difficult (*CW* 10.333 [review, de Girardin, first published 1850]).

State power

The creation of the middle class, first a means to break down feudalism, then a means to crush the emancipatory aspirations of the producers, of the working class (*Paris Commune* 150 [first draft, *Civil War in France,* written 1871]).
See also Class; State.

Stock   *See* Shares.

Stock exchange

Highest vocation for a capitalist, where property merges directly with theft (*Werke* 35.430 [to Bernstein, 10 February 1883 E]).
An institution where the bourgeoisie exploit not the workers but one another (*SC* 454 [to Bebel, 24 January 1893 E]).
Bourgeois confidence in any form of state only expresses itself in one way: by its quotation on the Stock Exchange (*CW* 10.503-4 [*May to October,* first published 1850]).
Hearth of extreme corruption (*SC* 454 [to Bebel, 24 January 1893 E]).
Excellent medium for the concentration of capitals, the disintegration and dissolution of the last remnants of naturally formed interconnections in bourgeois society and at the same time for the annihilation and conversion into their opposites of all orthodox moral conceptions (*SC* 454-5 [to Bebel, 24 January 1893 E]).
An incomparable element of destruction (*SC* 455 [to Bebel, 24 January 1893 E]).
A most powerful accelerator of the impending revolution (*SC* 455 [to Bebel, 24 January 1893 E]).

Structure (economic)

In the social production of their life, men enter into definite relations that are indispensable and independent of their will, relations of production which correspond to a definite stage of development of their material productive forces. The sum total of these relations of production constitutes the economic structure of society, the real foundation, on which rises a legal

and political superstructure and to which correspond definite forms of social consciousness (*SW* 181 [Preface to *Contribution to Critique of Political Economy*, first published 1859]).
See also Free trade; History; Society.

Subjects of labour

All those things which labour merely separates from immediate connexion with their environment (*Capital* 1.174; Penguin *Capital* 1.284).
See also Instrument of labour.
Part of the means of production (Penguin *Capital* 1.987).
Material in which the worker's labour manifests itself (Penguin *Capital* 1.988).
See also Means of production.

Subsumption (formal)

The labour-process becomes the instrument of the valorization process, the process of the self-valorization of capital – the manufacture of surplus-value. The labour process is subsumed under capital (it is its own process) and the capitalist intervenes in the process as its director, manager. For him it also represents the process as its director, manager. For him it also represents the direct exploitation of the labour of others. It is this that I refer to as the formal subsumption of labour under capital. It is the general form of every capitalist process of production (Penguin *Capital* 1.1019).
The form based on absolute surplus-value is what I call the formal subsumption of labour under capital (Penguin *Capital* 1.1025).

real subsumption

If the production of absolute surplus-value was the material expression of the formal subsumption of labour under capital, then the production of relative surplus-value may be viewed as its real subsumption (Penguin *Capital* 1.1025).
The real subsumption of labour under capital is developed in all the forms evolved by relative, as opposed to absolute surplus-value (Penguin *Capital* 1.1035).

Supersession

Supersession as an objective movement of retracting the alienation into self. This is the insight, expressed within the estrangement, concerning the appropriation of the objective essence through the supersession of its estrangement; it is the estranged insight into the real objectification of man, into the real appropriation of his objective essence through the annihilation of the estranged character of the objective world, through the supersession of the objective world in its estranged mode of being (*CW* 3.341 [*Economic and Philosophical Manuscripts*, written 1844]).

'Overcome and preserved'; overcome as regards form, and preserved as regards real content (*Anti-Dühring* 166 E).

Annihilated through criticism (*SW* 593 [*Ludwig Feuerbach*, first published 1886 E]).

See also Insurance fund; Property, private; Social capital.

Superstructure   *See* History; Revolution; Society, bourgeois; Structure (economic).

Supervision

The control exercised by the capitalist is not only a special function, due to the nature of the social labour-process, and peculiar to that process, but it is, at the same time, a function of the exploitation of a social labour-process, and is consequently rooted in the unavoidable antagonism between the exploiter and the living and labouring raw material he exploits. . . . If, then, the control of the capitalist is in substance two-fold by reason of the two-fold nature of the process of production itself – which, on the one hand, is a social process for producing use-values, on the other, a process for creating surplus-value – in form that control is despotic. As co-operation extends its scale, this despotism takes forms peculiar to itself. . . . It is not because he is a leader of industry that a man is a capitalist; on the contrary, he is a leader of industry because he is a capitalist. The leadership of industry is an attribute of capital, just as in feudal times the functions of general and judge, were attributes of landed property (*Capital* 1.313–15; Penguin *Capital* 1.449–51).

The labour of supervision and management, arising as it does out of an antithesis, out of the supremacy of capital over labour, and being therefore common to all modes of production based on class contradictions like the capitalist mode, is directly and inseparably connected, also under the capitalist system, with productive functions which all combined social labour assigns to individuals as their special tasks. The wages of an *epitropos*, or *régisseur*, as he was called in feudal France, are entirely divorced from profit and assume the form of wages for skilled labour whenever the business is operated on a sufficiently large scale to warrant paying for such a manager. . . . It has already been remarked by Mr. Ure that it is not the industrial capitalists, but the industrial managers who are 'the soul of our industrial system'. . . . The capitalist mode of production has brought matters to a point where the work of supervision, entirely divorced from the ownership of capital, is always readily obtainable. It has, therefore, come to be useless for the capitalist to perform it himself. . . . The capitalist has become no less redundant as a functionary in production. . . . On the basis of capitalist production a new swindle develops in stock enterprise with respect to wages of management, in that boards of numerous managers or directors are placed above the actual director, for whom supervision and management serve only as a pretext to plunder the stockholders and amass wealth (*Capital* 3.386–9; Penguin *Capital* 3.510–14).

Supplies

Supplies exist in three forms: in the form of productive capital, in the form of a fund for individual consumption, and in the form of a commodity-supply or commodity-capital. The supply in one form decreases relatively when it increases in another, although its quantity may increase absolutely in all three forms simultaneously (*Capital* 2.143; Penguin *Capital* 2.217).
See also Commodity-supply.

productive supply
Latent production fund (*Capital* 2.150; Penguin *Capital* 2.224).

Merely potential production capital (*Capital* 2.250; Penguin *Capital* 2.323).

Supply and demand   *See* Law.

Supply formation

Adam Smith entertained the splendid notion that the formation of a supply was a phenomenon peculiar to capitalist production. More recent economists, for instance Lalor, insist on the contrary that it declines with the development of capitalist production. Sismondi even regards it as one of the drawbacks of the latter. . . . Instead of a supply arising only upon and from the conversion of the product into a commodity, and of the consumption-supply into a commodity-supply, as Adam Smith wrongly imagines, this change of form, on the contrary, causes most violent crises in the economy of the producers during the transition from production for one's own needs to commodity production (*Capital* 2.142–3; Penguin *Capital* 2.217–18).

involuntary supply formation

Arises from, or is identical with, a stagnation of the circulation which is independent of the knowledge of the commodity-producer and thwarts his will (*Capital* 2.149; Penguin *Capital* 2.223).

Surplus   *See* Abundance.

Surplus-labour   *See* Labour.

Surplus product

The material existence of surplus-value, which in its turn only represents surplus labour (*Theories of Surplus Value* 3.247).
The portion of the product that represents the surplus-value . . . we call 'surplus-produce'. Just as the rate of surplus-value is determined by its relation, not to the sum total of the

capital, but to its variable part; in like manner, the relative quantity of surplus-produce is determined by the ratio that this produce bears, not to the remaining part of the total product, but to that part of it in which is incorporated the necessary labour. Since the production of surplus-value is the chief end and aim of capitalist production, it is clear, that the greatness of a man's or a nation's wealth should be measured, not by the absolute quantity produced, but by the relative magnitude of the surplus-produce (*Capital* 1.220; Penguin *Capital* 1.338–9).

That portion of the output which represents the total surplus-value, or in some cases that portion which represents the average profit (*Capital* 3.692; Penguin *Capital* 3.831).

Surplus-value

The relation of living labour to that objectified in the worker (Penguin *Grundrisse* 337).

The determining purpose, the driving force and the final result of the capitalist process of production (Penguin *Capital* 1.976).

Increment or excess over the original value (*Capital* 1.149; Penguin *Capital* 1.251).

The difference between the value of the product and the value of the elements consumed in the formation of that product, in other words, of the means of production and the labour-power (*Capital* 1.201; Penguin *Capital* 1.317).

The embodiment of unpaid labour (*Capital* 2.170; Penguin *Capital* 2.246).

Fund for supplying the individual consumption of the capitalist (*Capital* 1.554; Penguin *Capital* 1.738).

The excess over the cost-price (*Capital* 3.34; Penguin *Capital* 3.124).

Unpaid surplus labour (*Capital* 3.42; Penguin *Capital* 3.133).

The surplus-value created by the labourer is divided into revenue and capital; i.e. into articles of consumption and additional means of production (*Capital* 3.848; Penguin *Capital* 3.988).

See also Accumulation; Insurance fund; Law; Labour, living, productive; Price of production; Reproduction process; Shares; Surplus product; Working-day.

absolute surplus-value
Surplus-value produced by prolongation of the working-day (*Capital* 1.299; Penguin *Capital* 1.432).

forms of surplus-value
Profit, interest and ground-rent (*Capital* 3.595; Penguin *Capital* 3.730).

magnitude of surplus-value
Surplus value . . . is determined by the rate of surplus-value multiplied by the number of workers employed (*Theories of Surplus Value* 3.350–1).

production of absolute surplus-value
Prolongation of the working-day beyond the point at which the labourer would have produced just an equivalent for the value of his labour-power, and the appropriation of that surplus-labour by capital (*Capital* 1.477; Penguin *Capital* 1.645).
The general groundwork of the capitalist system, and the starting-point for the production of relative surplus-value (*Capital* 1.477; Penguin *Capital* 1.645).

rate of surplus-value
An exact expression for the degree of exploitation of labour-power by capital (*Capital* 1.209; Penguin *Capital* 1.326).

$\dfrac{\text{Surplus labour}}{\text{Necessary labour}}$ (*Capital* 1.209; Penguin *Capital* 1.326).

The ratio of the variable capital employed during a definite period to the surplus-value produced in the same time; or the quantity of unpaid labour set in motion by the variable capital employed during this time. It has absolutely nothing to do with that portion of the variable capital which is advanced during the time in which it is not employed (*Capital* 2.308; Penguin *Capital* 2.379).
Division of the value of the product between the capitalist and the worker (*Theories of Surplus Value* 2.21).
The ratio of the total surplus-value produced during one year to the sum of value of the advanced variable capital is . . . the

annual rate of surplus-value (*Capital* 2.299; Penguin *Capital* 2.371).

relative surplus-value

Surplus-value arising from the curtailment of the necessary labour-time, and from the corresponding alteration in the respective lengths of the two components of the working-day (*Capital* 1.299; Penguin *Capital* 1.432).

Surplus-value insofar as it arises out of the growing productivity of labour (*Theories of Surplus Value* 2.16).

Relative surplus-value is absolute, since it compels the absolute prolongation of the working-day beyond the labour-time necessary to the existence of the labourer himself. Absolute surplus-value is relative, since it makes necessary such a development of the productiveness of labour, as will allow of the necessary labour-time being confined to a portion of the working-day. But if we keep in mind the behaviour of surplus-value, this appearance of identity vanishes (*Capital* 1.478–9; Penguin *Capital* 1.646).

System *See* Division of labour, social; Mode of production.

system of social estates

Form of political constitution representing the 'social' interests of the feudal aristocracy, the bureaucracy and the monarchy by the grace of God (*CW* 8.263 [*Montesquieu*, first published 1849]).

T

Tariffs

Customs duties originated from the tributes which the feudal lords exacted from merchants passing through their territories as protection money against robbery, tributes later imposed likewise by the towns, and which, with the rise of the modern states, were the Treasury's most obvious means of raising money (*CW* 5.70 [*German Ideology*, written 1845–6]).
See also Free-trade, and protectionism.

Taxes

Economic existence of the state (*CW* 6.329 [*Moralizing Criticism*, first published 1847]).
Source of life for the bureaucracy, the army, the priests and the court, in short, for the whole apparatus of the executive power (*CW* 11.191 [*Eighteenth Brumaire*, first published 1852]).
Economic basis of the government machinery and of nothing else (*SW* 328 [*Critique of the Gotha Programme*, written 1875]).

Technology   *See* Relations, economic.

Temperate zone

Mother country of capitalist production (*Capital* 2.159; Penguin *Capital* 2.236).

Tenant farmers

The tenant farmer is the landowner's representative – the landowner's revealed secret (*CW* 3.286 [*Economic and Philosophical Manuscripts*, written 1844]).

Theory of value

The value of every commodity – thus also of the commodities making up the capital – is determined not by the necessary labour-time contained in it, but by the social labour-time required for its reproduction (*Capital* 3.141; Penguin *Capital* 3.238).

After the abolition of the capitalist mode of production, but still retaining social production, the determination of value continues to prevail in the sense that the regulation of labour-time and the distribution of social labour among the various production groups, ultimately the book-keeping encompassing all this, become more essential than ever (*Capital* 3.851; Penguin *Capital* 3.991).

See also Law.

Time

The room of human development (*SW* 219 [*Wages, Price and Profit*, written 1865]).

If in commerce time is money, in warfare time is victory (*CW* 14.349 [*Russell's Resignation*, first published 1855]).

Measure of labour (Penguin *Grundrisse* 613).

See also Accumulation; Material space.

Time-wages

The converted form under which the daily, weekly etc. value of labour-power presents itself (*Capital* 1.508; Penguin *Capital* 1.683).

See also Wage-labour.

Tool

Specific human activity, the transforming reaction of man on nature, production (*Dialectics of Nature* 47 E).

Total labour   *See* Labour, total.

Totality   *See* Production; Proletariat; Property, private.

Town

contradiction between town and country

The contradiction between town and country begins with the transition from barbarism to civilization, from tribe to state, from locality to nation, and runs through the whole history of civilization to the present day (the Anti-Corn Law League). The advent of the town implies, at the same time, the necessity of administration, police, taxes, etc., in short, of the municipality, and thus of politics in general. Here first became manifest the division of the population into two great classes, which is directly based on the division of labour and on the instruments of production. The town is in actual fact already the concentration of the population, of the instruments of production, of capital, of pleasures, of needs, while the country demonstrates just the opposite fact, isolation and separation. The contradiction between town and country can only exist within the framework of private property. It is the most crass expression of the subjection of the individual under the division of labour, under a definite activity forced upon him – a subjection which makes one man into a restricted town-animal, another into a restricted country-animal, and daily creates anew the conflict between their interests. Labour is here again the chief thing, power *over* individuals, and as long as this power exists, private property must exist. The abolition of the contradiction between town and country is one of the first conditions of communal life, a condition which again depends on a mass of material premises and which cannot be fulfilled by the mere will, as anyone can see at the first glance. (These conditions have still to be set forth.) The separation of town and country can also be understood as the separation of capital and landed property, as the beginning of the existence and development of capital independent of landed property – the beginning of property having its basis only in labour and exchange (*CW* 5.64 [*German Ideology*, written 1845–6]).

Trade

The exchange of products of various individuals and countries (*CW* 5.48 [*German Ideology*, written 1845–6]).

Commerce is both historically as well as conceptually a pre-supposition for the rise of capital (Penguin *Grundrisse* 672).

The product becomes a commodity by way of commerce. It is commerce which here turns products into commodities, not the produced commodity which by its movements gives rise to commerce (*Capital* 3.328; Penguin *Capital* 3.445).

Originally trade is the pre-condition for the transformation of guild, rural domestic and feudal agricultural production into capitalist production. It develops the product into a commodity, partly by creating a market for it, partly by giving rise to new commodity equivalents and partly by supplying production with new materials and thereby initiating new kinds of production which are based on trade from the very beginning because they depend both on production for the market and on elements of production derived from the world market (*Theories of Surplus Value* 3.470).

See also Foreign trade; Relations, international; Weaving.

Transport

The transport industry forms on the one hand an independent branch of production and thus a separate sphere of investment of productive capital. On the other hand its distinguishing feature is that it appears as a continuation of a process of production within the process of circulation and for the process of circulation (*Capital* 2.155; Penguin *Capital* 2.229).

process of transportation

The productive process of the transport industry (*Capital* 2.54; Penguin *Capital* 2.135).

Tribal property

The first form of property, in the ancient world as in the Middle Ages, is tribal property, determined with the Romans chiefly by war, with the Germans by the rearing of cattle (*CW* 5.89 [*German Ideology*, written 1845–6]).

Truth

Man must prove the truth, i.e. the reality and power, the this-worldliness of his thinking in practice (*CW* 5.3 [*Theses on Feuerbach*, written 1845]).

Turnover

turnover of capital

A circuit performed by a capital and meant to be a periodical process, not an individual act (*Capital* 2.158; Penguin *Capital* 2.235).

turnover of merchant capital

The first phase in the metamorphosis of a commodity, as the refluent movement of a specific capital (*Capital* 3.302; Penguin *Capital* 3.417).
See also Number of turnovers (of total social capital); Periods of turnover.

Turnover-time

Time of production plus time of circulation; measures the interval of time between one circuit period of the entire capital-value and the next, the periodicity in the process of life of capital or, if you like, the time of the renewal, the repetition, of the process of self-expansion, or production, of one and the same capital-value. . . . From the point of view of the capitalist, the time of turnover of his capital is the time for which he must advance his capital in order to create surplus-value with it and receive it back in its original shape (*Capital* 2.158–9; Penguin *Capital* 2.235–6).

U

Unproductive costs

The existence of capital in its form of commodity-capital and hence of commodity-supply gives rise to costs which must be classed as costs of circulation, since they do not come within the sphere of production. . . . The capital and labour-power which serve the need of preserving and storing the commodity-supply are withdrawn from the direct process of production. On the other hand the capitals thus employed, including labour-power as a constituent of capital, must be replaced out of the social product. Their expenditure has therefore the effect of diminishing the productive power of labour, so that a greater amount of capital and labour is required to obtain a particular useful effect. They are unproductive costs (*Capital* 2.141–2; Penguin *Capital* 2.216).

A part of the social wealth that must be sacrificed to the process of circulation (*Capital* 2.139; Penguin *Capital* 2.214).

Costs which enhance the price of a commodity without adding to its use-value, which therefore are to be classed as unproductive expenses so far as society is concerned, may be a source of enrichment to the individual capitalist. On the other hand, as this addition to the price of the commodity merely distributes these costs of circulation equally, they do not thereby cease to be unproductive in character. For instance insurance companies divide the losses of individual capitalists among the capitalist class. But this does not prevent these equalized losses from remaining losses so far as the aggregate social capital is concerned (*Capital* 2.140; Penguin *Capital* 2.214–15).

Use-value

Whatever its social form may be, wealth always consists of use-values, which in the first instance are not affected by this form (*Contribution to Critique of Political Economy* 27–8).

The immediate physical entity in which a definite economic relationship – exchange-value – is expressed (*Contribution to Critique of Political Economy* 28).

The concrete form in which commodities enter the process of exchange (*Contribution to Critique of Political Economy* 68).

Object of satisfaction of any system whatever of human needs (Penguin *Grundrisse* 881).

The content, the natural particularity of the commodity (Penguin *Grundrisse* 267).

Production for direct consumption (Penguin *Grundrisse* 502).

The bodies of commodities (*Capital* 1.50; Penguin *Capital* 1.133).

Combinations of two elements – matter and labour (*Capital* 1.50; Penguin *Capital* 1.133).

Basis of the exchange-value of a commodity (*Capital* 3.636; Penguin *Capital* 3.774).

See also Abundance; Capacity for labour.

use-value and exchange-value

Exchange-value expresses the social form of value, while use-value [is] no economic form of it whatever, rather, merely the being of the product, etc. for mankind generally (Penguin *Grundrisse* 872).

Selling in order to purchase is the principle of use value; purchasing in order to sell is that of value (*Grundrisse* 929).

Usurer's capital

Antiquated form of interest-bearing capital (*Capital* 3.593; Penguin *Capital* 3.728).

Usurer's capital employs the method of exploitation characteristic of capital yet without the latter's mode of production (*Capital* 3.597; Penguin *Capital* 3.732).

usurer's capital and interest-bearing capital

The credit system develops as a reaction against usury. But this should not be misunderstood, nor by any means interpreted in the manner of the ancient writers, the church fathers, Luther or the early socialists. It signifies no more and no less than the subordination of interest-bearing capital to the conditions and requirements of the capitalist mode of production.

On the whole, interest-bearing capital under the modern credit system is adapted to the conditions of the capitalist mode of production. Usury as such does not only continue to exist, but is even freed, among nations with a developed capitalist production, from the fetters imposed upon it by all previous legislation. Interest-bearing capital retains the form of usurer's capital in relation to persons or classes, or in circumstances where borrowing does not, nor can, take place in the sense corresponding to the capitalist mode of production. . . . What distinguishes interest-bearing capital – in so far as it is an essential element of the capitalist mode of production – from usurer's capital is by no means the nature or character of this capital itself. It is merely the altered conditions under which it operates, and consequently also the totally transformed character of the borrower who confronts the moneylender (*Capital* 3.600; Penguin *Capital* 3.735).

usurer's capital and merchant capital

The middle ages had handed down two distinct forms of capital, which mature in the most different economic social formations, and which, before the era of the capitalist mode of production, are considered as capital *quand même* – usurer's capital and merchant's capital (*Capital* 1.702; Penguin *Capital* 1.914).

Usury

The inevitable companion of a class of free small peasants (*CW* 7.330).

Usury is a powerful lever in developing the preconditions for industrial capital in so far as it plays the following double role, first, building up, in general, an independent money wealth alongside that of the merchant, and, secondly, appropriating the conditions of labour, that is, ruining the owners of the old conditions of labour (*Capital* 3.610; Penguin *Capital* 3.745).

V

Valorization process   *See* Realization process.

Value

The relation of production costs to utility (*CW* 3.426; [*Outlines*, first published 1844 E]).

A generality, in which all individuality and peculiarity are negated and extinguished (Penguin *Grundrisse* 157).

Forms the foundation of capital (Penguin *Grundrisse* 421).

The concept of value is entirely peculiar to the most modern economy, since it is the most abstract expression of capital itself and of the production resting on it. In the concept of value, its secret betrayed (Penguin *Grundrisse* 776).

A use-value, or useful article, therefore, has value only because human labour in the abstract has been embodied or materialized in it (*Capital* 1.46; Penguin *Capital* 1.129).

The real value of a commodity is, however, not its individual value, but its social value; that is to say, the real value is not measured by the labour-time that the article in each individual case costs the producer, but by the labour-time socially required for its production (*Capital* 1.301; Penguin *Capital* 1.434).

The objective form of the social labour expended in its production (*Capital* 1.501; Penguin *Capital* 1.675).

The centre of gravity around which the prices of commodities fluctuate (*Capital* 3.178; Penguin *Capital* 3.279).

Not determined by the labour-time originally expended in their production, but by the labour-time expended in their reproduction (*Capital* 3.398; Penguin *Capital* 3.522).

The expression of the socially necessary human labour materialized in an object (*Anti-Dühring* 238 E).

The 'Verbal Observer', Bailey, and others remark that 'value', '*valeur*' express a property of things. In fact the terms originally express but the use-value of things for people, those qualities which make them useful or agreeable etc. to people. It is in the nature of things that 'value', '*valeur*', '*Wert*' can have no other etymological origin. Use-value expresses the natural relationship between things and men, in fact the existence of things for men. Exchange-value, as the result of the social development which created it, was later superimposed on the word value, which was synonymous with use-value. It [exchange-value] is the social existence of things.

The Sanskrit – *Wer* [means] cover, protect, consequently respect, honour and love, cherish. From these the adjective *Wertas* (excellent, respectable) is derived; Gothic, *wairths*, Old German, Old Frankish, *wert*; Anglo-Saxon, *weorth*, *vordh*, *wurth*; English, worth, worthy; Dutch, *waard*, *waaridg*; Alemanic, *werth*; Lithuanian, *wertas* (respectable, precious, dear, estimable).

The Sanskrit, *wertis*; Latin, *virtus*; Gothic, *wairthi*; German, *Werth*. The value of a thing is, in fact, its own virtue, while its exchange-value is quite independent of its material qualities (*Theories of Surplus Value* 3.296–7).

See also Labour-power; Law; Price of production; Productivity; Self-expansion of value; Theory of value.

differential value

Difference between market value and individual value (*Theories of Surplus Value* 2.268).

equivalent form of value

Character of direct and universal exchangeability (*Capital* 1.75; Penguin *Capital* 1.162).

First peculiarity: use-value becomes the form of manifestation, the phenomenal form of its opposite, value. . . . Second peculiarity: concrete labour becomes the form under which its opposite, abstract human labour, manifests itself. . . . Third peculiarity: the labour of private individuals takes the form of its opposite, labour directly social in its form (*Capital* 1.62–4; Penguin *Capital* 1.148–51).

market value

Centre of fluctuation for market-prices (*Capital* 3.178; Penguin *Capital* 3.279).

Determined by the value of the commodities produced under average conditions (*Capital* 3.182; Penguin *Capital* 3.283).

value and price

Magnitude of value expresses a relation of social production, it expresses the connexion that necessarily exists between a certain article and the portion of the total labour-time of society required to produce it. As soon as magnitude of value is converted into price, the above necessary relation takes the shape of a more or less accidental exchange-ratio between a single commodity and another, the money-commodity. But this exchange-ratio may express either the real magnitude of that commodity's value, or the quantity of gold deviating from that value, for which, according to circumstances, it may be parted with. The possibility, therefore, of quantitative incongruity between price and magnitude of value, or the deviation of the former from the latter, is inherent in the price-form itself. . . . The price-form, however, is not only compatible with the possibility of a quantitative incongruity between magnitude of value and price, i.e. between the former and its expression in money, but it may also conceal a qualitative inconsistency, so much so, that, although money is nothing but the value-form of commodities, price ceases altogether to express value. Objects that in themselves are no commodities, such as conscience, honour, etc. are capable of being offered for sale by their holders, and of thus acquiring, through their price, the form of commodities. Hence an object may have a price without having value. The price in that case is imaginary, like certain quantities in mathematics (*Capital* 1.104–5; Penguin *Capital* 1.196–7).

value of labour-power   *See* Labour-power.

value of variable capital

Average value of one labour-power, multiplied by the number of labour-powers employed (*Capital* 1.287; Penguin *Capital* 1.417).

Value-creation

Determined not simply by the labour employed during the immediate production process, but by the degree to which this exploitation of labour can be repeated within a given period time (Penguin *Grundrisse* 741).

See also Process of creating value.

Value-form (of the labour-product)

The most abstract but also the most universal form taken by the product in bourgeois production, and it stamps that production as a particular species of social production, and thereby gives it its special historical character (*Capital* 1.85; Penguin *Capital* 1.174).

Velocity (of money)

The number of moves made by a given piece of money in a given time (*Capital* 1.121; Penguin *Capital* 1.216).

W

Wage-labour

The condition for capital (*CW* 6.496 [*Communist Manifesto*, first published 1848]).

In the strict economic sense, . . . capital-positing, capital-producing labour, i.e. living labour which produces both the objective conditions of its realization as an activity, as well as the objective moments of its being as labour capacity, and produces them as alien powers opposite itself, as values for themselves, independent of it (Penguin *Grundrisse* 463).

Essential mediating form of capitalist relations of production, and constantly reproduced by those relations themselves (Penguin *Capital* 1.1064).

Basis on which the production of products as commodities takes place (*Theories of Surplus Value* 2.397).

See also Bourgeoisie; Wages system.

Wages

Direct consequence of estranged labour (*CW* 3.280 [*Economic and Philosophical Manuscripts*, written 1844]).

Special name for the price of labour, for the price of this peculiar commodity which has no other repository than human flesh and blood (*CW* 9.201 [*Wage Labour and Capital*, first published 1849]).

Not the workers' share in the commodity produced by him. Wages are the part of already existing commodities with which the capitalist buys for himself a definite amount of productive labour (*CW* 9.202 [*Wage Labour and Capital*, first published 1849]).

The price of necessary labour (Penguin *Grundrisse* 570).

The money-form in which the variable capital is advanced (*Capital* 2.330; Penguin *Capital* 2.401).

Form of the value of labour-power (*Capital* 2.375; Penguin *Capital* 2.447).

Specific form of revenue (*Capital* 3.833; Penguin *Capital* 3.972).

The materialisation of that portion of the total working-day of the labourer in which the value of variable capital and thus the price of labour is reproduced (*Capital* 3.833; Penguin *Capital* 3.972).

Portion of commodity-value in which the labourer reproduces the value of his own labour-power, or the price of his labour (*Capital* 3.833; Penguin *Capital* 3.972).

Value of variable capital (*Theories of Surplus Value* 1.395).

See also Means of life; Piece-wages; Time-wages.

The product of the exchange between worker and capital (Penguin *Grundrisse* 294).

Not a constituent element of production. It is an accident, a form of our state of society (Penguin *Grundrisse* 592).

In the hand of the worker, the wage is no longer a wage, but a consumption fund. It is wages only in the hand of the capitalist, i.e. the part of capital destined to be exchanged for labour-capacity (Penguin *Grundrisse* 594).

The equivalent with which the capitalist buys the temporary disposal of labour-power (*Theories of Surplus Value* 1.86).

nominal wages

Money price of labour (*CW* 9.217 [*Wage Labour and Capital*, first published 1849]).

Wages estimated in value (*Capital* 1.508; Penguin *Capital* 1.683).

Equivalent of labour-power expressed in money (*Capital* 1.525; Penguin *Capital* 1.702).

real wages

The quantity of use-values received by the labourer for the same quantity of labour (*Capital* 3.861; Penguin *Capital* 3.1001).

Sum of commodities which is actually given in exchange for wages (*CW* 9.217 [*Wage Labour and Capital*, first published 1849]).

Wages as measured by the quantity of the commodities they can buy (*SW* 185 [*Wages, Price and Profit*, written 1865]).

Means of subsistence placed at the disposal of the labourer (*Capital* 1.525; Penguin *Capital* 1.702).

relative wages

Relative wages express the price of direct labour in relation to the price of accumulated labour, the relative value of wage-labour and capital, the reciprocal value of the capitalist and worker (*CW* 9.218 [*Wage Labour and Capital*, first published 1849]).

Wages in relation to profit (*Werke* 28.615 [to Lassalle, 23 January 1855]).

See also Price of labour, relative.

Wages system

Wage-labour.

Social form of work indispensable to capitalist production. Necessary condition for the formation of capital (Penguin *Capital* 1.1006).

War

War is the great comprehensive task, the great communal labour which is required either to occupy the objective conditions of being there alive, or to protect and perpetuate the occupation (Penguin *Grundrisse* 474).

Warfare is therefore one of the earliest occupations of each of these naturally arisen communities, both for the defence of their property and for obtaining new property (Penguin *Grundrisse* 491).

See also Competition; Supervision; Tribal property.

Wealth

Wealth is on one side a thing, realized in things, material products, which a human being confronts as subject; on the other side, as value, wealth is merely command over alien labour not with the aim of ruling, but with the aim of private consumption etc. It appears in all forms in the shape of a thing, be it an object or be it a relation mediated through the object, which is external and accidental to the individual. Thus the old view, in which the human being appears as the aim of production, regardless of his limited national, religious, political character, seems to be very lofty when contrasted to the modern world, where production appears as the aim of mankind and wealth as the aim of production. In fact, however, when the limited bourgeois form is stripped away, what is wealth other than the universality of individual needs, capacities, pleasures, productive forces etc., created through universal exchange? The full development of human mastery over the forces of nature, those of so-called nature as well as of humanity's own nature? The absolute working-out of his creative potentialities, with no presupposition other than the previous historic development, which makes this totality of development, i.e. the development of all human powers as such the end in itself, not as measured on a *predetermined* yardstick? Where he does not reproduce himself in one specificity, but produces his totality? Strives not to remain something he has become, but is in the absolute movement of becoming? In bourgeois economics – and in the epoch of production to which it corresponds – this complete working-out of the human content appears as a complete emptying-out, this universal objectification as total alienation, and the tearing-down of all limited, one-sided aims as sacrifice of the human end-in-itself to an entirely external end. This is why the childish world of antiquity appears on one side as loftier. On the other side, it really is loftier in all matters where closed shapes, forms and given limits are sought for. It is satisfaction from a limited standpoint; while the modern gives no satisfaction; or, where it appears satisfied with itself, it is *vulgar* (Penguin *Grundrisse* 487-8).

Immense accumulation of commodities (*Capital* 1.43; Penguin *Capital* 1.125).

The formation of capital and the reckless exploitation and impoverishing of the mass of the people (*Capital* 1.673; Penguin *Capital* 1.879).

national wealth

Identical with misery of the people (*Capital* 1.722; Penguin *Capital* 1.938).

real wealth

The developed productive power of all individuals (Penguin *Grundrisse* 708).

social wealth

The wealth of society exists only as the wealth of private individuals, who are its private owners. It preserves its social character only in that these individuals mutually exchange qualitatively different use-values for the satisfaction of their wants. Under capitalist production they can do so only by means of money. Thus the wealth of the individual is realized as social wealth only through the medium of money. It is in money, in this thing, that the social nature of this wealth is incarnated (*Capital* 3.573 E; Penguin *Capital* 3.707 E).
See also Commodity; Proletariat.

Wear and tear

By wear and tear (moral depreciation excepted) is meant that part of value which the fixed capital, on being used, gradually transmits to the product, in proportion to its average loss of use-value (*Capital* 2.174; Penguin *Capital* 2.250).

material and moral wear and tear

The material wear and tear of a machine is of two kinds. The one arises from use, as coins wear away by circulating, the other from non-use, as a sword rusts when left in its scabbard. The latter kind is due to the elements. The former is more or less directly proportional, the latter to a certain extent inversely proportional, to the use of the machine.

But in addition to the material wear and tear, a machine also undergoes, what we may call a moral depreciation. It loses exchange-value, either by machines of the same sort being produced cheaper than it, or by better machines entering into competition with it. In both cases, be the machine ever so young and full of life, its value is no longer determined by the labour actually materialized in it, but by the labour-time requisite to reproduce either it or the better machine. It has, therefore, lost value more or less. The shorter the period taken to reproduce its total value, the less is the danger of moral depreciation, and the longer the working-day, the shorter is that period. When machinery is first introduced into an industry new methods of reproducing it more cheaply follow blow upon blow, and so do improvements, that not only affect individual parts and details of the machine, but its entire build. It is, therefore, in the early days of the life of machinery that this special incentive to the prolongation of the working-day makes itself felt more acutely (*Capital* 1.381–2; Penguin *Capital* 1.528).

Weaving

Weaving, earlier carried on in the country by the peasants as a secondary occupation to procure their clothing, was the first labour to receive an impetus and a further development through the extension of intercourse. Weaving was the first and remained the principal manufacture. . . . Alongside the peasants weaving for their own use, who continued, and still continue, with this sort of work, there emerged a new class of weavers in the towns, whose fabrics were destined for the whole home market and usually for foreign markets too (*CW* 5.68 [*German Ideology*, written 1845–6]).

Women

The collecting of persons of both sexes and all ages in a single work-room, the inevitable contact, the crowding into a small space of people, to whom neither mental nor moral education has been given, is not calculated for the favourable develop-ment of the female character. . . . It is, besides, a matter of course that factory servitude, like any other, and to an even higher degree, confers the *jus primae noctis* upon the master. In this respect also the employer is sovereign over the persons and charms of his employees. The threat of discharge suffices to overcome all resistance in nine cases out of ten, if not in ninety-nine out of a hundred (*CW* 4.441–2 [*Condition of the Working Class*, first published 1845 E]).

The standardization of the working day must include the restriction of female labour, in so far as it relates to the dura-tion, intermissions, etc., of the working day; otherwise 'restriction' could only mean the exclusion of female labour from branches of industry that are especially unhealthy for the female body or are objectionable morally for the female sex. If that is what was meant [in the Gotha Programme], it should have been said so (*SW* 330 [*Critique of the Gotha Programme*, written 1875]).

The emancipation of women becomes possible only when women are enabled to take part in production on a large, social scale, and when domestic duties require their attention only to a minor degree. And this has become possible only as a result of a modern large-scale industry, which not only permits of the participation of women in production in large numbers, but actually calls for it and, moreover, strives to convert private domestic work also into a public industry (*SW* 569–70 [*Family, Private Property, State*, first published 1884 E]). *See also* Community of women.

Worker   *See* Labourer; Proletarian.

Workhouses

A Malthusian deterrent against pauperism (*CW* 5.366 [*German Ideology*, written 1845–6]).
Device for maintaining a reserve army in readiness for favourable periods while converting them in these pious institutions during unfavourable commercial periods into machines devoid of will, resistance, claims and requirements (*CW* 8.219 [*Bourgeois Document*, first published 1849]).
Place of punishment for misery (*Capital* 1.612; Penguin *Capital* 1.808).

Working-day

The sum of the necessary labour and the surplus-labour, i.e. of the periods of time during which the workman replaces the value of his labour-power, and produces the surplus-value (*Capital* 1.221; Penguin *Capital* 1.339).
The absolute extent of the worker's labour-time (*Capital* 1.221; Penguin *Capital* 1.339).
The natural unit for measuring the function of labour-power (*Capital* 2.159; Penguin *Capital* 2.236).

shortening of the working day   *See* Freedom.

Working-period

A more or less numerous succession of connected working-days (*Capital* 2.234; Penguin *Capital* 2.308).
The period necessary to get the product ready for the market (*Capital* 2.320; Penguin *Capital* 2.391).

Working-period and working-day

When we speak of a working-day we mean the length of working time during which the labourer must daily spend his labour-power, must work day by day. But when we speak of a working-period we mean the number of connected working-days required in a certain branch of industry for the manufacture of a finished product. In this case the product of every working-day is but a partial one, which is further worked upon from day to day and only at the end of the longer or shorter working-period receives its finished form, is a finished use-value (*Capital* 2.234; Penguin *Capital* 2.308).

World market   *See* Market.

INDEX